ALL NATIONS UNDER GOD

All Nations Under God

The Doctrine of
Christ's Victorious Atonement:
Defined, Defended,
and Applied

Published by:

The Armoury Ministries
www.thearmouryministries.com

All Nations Under God

*Unless otherwise indicated,
all Scripture references are taken from the New American Standard Bible,
Copyright © 1960, 1962, 1963, 1968, 1971, 1972, 1973,
1975, 1977, 1995 by The Lockman Foundation
Used by permission. (www.lockman.org)*

*Scripture quotations marked "NKJV" are taken from the New King James Version.
Copyright © 1982 by Thomas Nelson, Inc. Used by permission. All rights reserved.*

*Scripture quotations marked (NIV) are taken from the HOLY BIBLE, NEW INTERNATIONAL VERSION®.
NIV®. Copyright©1973, 1978, 1984 by International Bible Society. Used by permission of Zondervan. All rights reserved.*

*Scripture quotations marked "NCV™" are taken from the New Century Version®.
Copyright © 2005 by Thomas Nelson, Inc. Used by permission. All rights reserved.*

*All Nations Under God
ISBN: 978-1-935358-03-9
Copyright © 2005 by Michael J. Beasley.*

Library of Congress Cataloging-in-Publication Data

Michael John Beasley

    All Nations Under God
    Includes bibliographical references and index.
    Library of Congress Registration: TX 6-223-550
    DREG: 23RD AUGUST 2005

All rights reserved. No part of this book may be reproduced, stored in a retrieval system, or transmitted in any form or by any means – electronic, mechanical, photocopy, recording, or otherwise – without written permission of the publisher, except for brief quotations in printed reviews. For more information go to: www.thearmouryministries.org.

⇒ *Dedication* ⇐

In memory of

Dr. John Owen

1616-1683,

with thanks to all those saints,

living and asleep in Jesus,

whose godly friendship and

support has aided me

throughout

the years

ALL NATIONS UNDER GOD

CONTENTS

INTRODUCING THE GREATEST STORY EVER TOLD 11
    The Greatest Story Ever Told
    The Tragedy of Traditions
    Why "Victorious" Atonement?
    An Agenda Of Adoration

CHRIST'S VICTORIOUS ATONEMENT DEFINED 27
    For Whom Did Christ Die?
    The Intent of Christ's Atonement
    The Immutability of Christ's Atonement
    The Extent of Christ's Atonement

CHRIST'S VICTORIOUS ATONEMENT DEFENDED 51

A Defense, Not a Diatribe
A Defense of The Lord's Justice & Mercy
A Defense of the Lord's Exceptional Love
A Defense of the Lord's Extensive Atonement
"Victory" Means "Victory" All Of the Time

CHRIST'S VICTORIOUS ATONEMENT APPLIED 89

Listening to the Victorious Lamb
The Greatest of these is Love
The Exceptional Love Of A Husband
The Exceptional Love Of A Wife
The Exceptional Love Of Heaven's Citizens
The Exceptional Love Of The Brethren
The Exceptional Love Of God's Messengers
Following The Victorious Lamb

CHRIST'S TRIUMPH OVER TRADITION 117

Christ's Triumph Over Tradition
The Trauma Of Tradition
The Tradition of Free Will
The Tradition of Hypercalvinism
The Tradition of Unexceptional Love
The Tradition Of "Whosoever"
There Are Foolish Men On Both Sides Of The Argument

CELEBRATING HIS VICTORY FOR ALL ETERNITY 135

Fixing Our Eyes On Jesus
His Holy And Eternal Victory
Adoring The Lamb of God Forever

APPENDIX – RIGHTLY DIVIDING THE WORD 145

Revelation 21:1-6

1 And I saw a new heaven and a new earth; for the first heaven and the first earth passed away, and there is no longer any sea. 2 And I saw the holy city, new Jerusalem, coming down out of heaven from God, made ready as a bride adorned for her husband. 3 And I heard a loud voice from the throne, saying, "Behold, the tabernacle of God is among men, and He shall dwell among them, and they shall be His people, and God Himself shall be among them, 4 and He shall wipe away every tear from their eyes; and there shall no longer be any death; there shall no longer be any mourning, or crying, or pain; the first things have passed away." 5 And He who sits on the throne said, "Behold, I am making all things new." And He *said, "Write, for these words are faithful and true." 6 And He said to me, "It is done.

I am the Alpha and the Omega, the beginning and the end.

I will give to the one who thirsts

from the spring of the water of life

without cost."

ALL NATIONS UNDER GOD

INTRODUCING THE GREATEST STORY

EVER TOLD

The Greatest Story Ever Told

And she will bear a Son; and you shall call His name Jesus, for it is He who will save His people from their sins.
Matthew 1:21

There is no greater story in the Universe – *Jesus Christ, the Lamb of God, offered up His own life as a sacrifice to save His people from their sins!* This precious doctrine of Christ's atoning sacrifice is the only ray of hope within this dark and despairing world. It offers the explosive message of true joy through the forgiveness of sin. It tells us that we can be mercifully delivered from the wrath of God through faith in Christ. It assures the genuine believer that he will not suffer eternal torment in the depths of a fiery hell, and in eternal glory, the reigning theme of worship will center on the worthy Lamb of God who receives all power, riches, wisdom, might, honor, glory, and blessing!

Yet sadly, this doctrine also happens to be one of the most *contentious* issues in the modern church!

It is a perplexing matter of reflection, but it is true - what should be a loudly celebrated message of the church has become the basis of a torrid battle. In recent years the doctrine of the atonement has been placed at the center of an aggressive tug-of-war, fueled by many emotional and undisciplined arguments; and while there are those who are making a sound defense of their views by means of godly discourse and sound reasoning from the Scriptures, there are unfortunately many others whose tactics are quite foolish, and sometimes even cruel. Amidst it all, the Devil's tactics of distracting many in the church from this key Scriptural truth seem to be taking root. Because of this, the atoning work of Christ is becoming yet another key doctrine that is being stored in the preacher's closet for the sake of "unity" and "peace." But as it is with any compromise, such *unity* and *peace* is a mere phantom. By avoiding this central gem in the crown of God's revelation, the church is choosing to endure a deadly famine rather than thrive at that rich feast which celebrates the greatest work of the Savior. And instigating this anemia, beneath a false pretense of *truth*, are those who stir animosity and fear among the brethren, resulting in unrest and division in the local church. What I share here, concerning the contemporary church's conflict over the atonement, is not some remote concept or theory. Throughout my years in the ministry I have repeatedly faced this battle myself; hence, this is a fairly personal matter. Some of the most pugnacious encounters I have ever experienced were brought about by professing Christians who heralded certain pet arguments over the atonement – *with a vengeance*. While the church must never oppose open discourse and debate over important doctrines of the Bible, it must never tolerate those who wrangle over words while wielding their debate as a self serving weapon of destruction. I should also mention that the theological sources of such contention are often multifaceted. But whatever the source of such contention may be, all such wrangling amounts to a graceless and non-productive divisiveness which robs the church of her credibility and ministry. Rather than avoiding such matters altogether, the church of Jesus Christ must rise above such divisive immaturity. She must not malign nor ignore the greatest story ever told; to do so would be tantamount to the pharisaical error of *setting aside* God's word. In light of these great dangers, let me offer a needful word of warning concerning the *tragedy of traditions*, just as our Savior often did when teaching His disciples.

THE TRAGEDY OF TRADITIONS

*"You nicely set aside the commandment of God
in order to keep your tradition."*
Mark 7:9

I have had the privilege of serving as a pastor for many years, and have visited several churches in various portions of the Pacific, Midwest, and Eastern United States. In my experience in ministry, I have found that the American church is rife with many dangerous influences: the emasculation of men, the advancement of feminism, the import of secularism, the adoration of programs over spirituality, the neglect of expository preaching, and with that *the avoidance of core doctrines* - along with a host of other issues. But all of these matters have a root source; a bad seed if you will, which makes one wonder how much of the modern church is actually – *the church.* This bad seed to which I refer is a rebellion against the authority of God. Thinking of it all in another way - a church that is submitting to the authority of Christ will have men and women who gladly embrace their biblical roles; it will look to root out worldliness while heralding genuine spirituality in its programs and activities; and ultimately, such a submissive church will herald all of the doctrines of Scripture rather than hiding some of them in shame. The churches in this nation that are characterized by this godly submission to God's Word are vastly outnumbered by those that proudly herald a different authority; such a consideration as this is alarming! As a Christian first, and as an undershepherd of Christ's church, my heart has been deeply grieved by the discovery of these frequent problems. Time and time again I have witnessed the tragedy which comes when the authority of God's Word is undermined, but in a manner that is rarely detected in this modern era. In 2002 I began considering a call to a *Bible* church. This inaugurated a process that involved a number of conference calls, e-mails, and personal visits to the church over the span of several months. Elders, deacons, the search committee, and even the whole church all had full access to over 50 pages of documentation outlining my doctrinal convictions as well as my philosophies of ministry and worship. Needless to say, there was *nothing hidden* concerning my Scriptural convictions! When I had the chance to visit this church, in order to preach and meet with its members, I found a fairly broad sampling of views among the people. As I had experienced in many other churches before, there was a mixture of those who were willing to open the Bible and have a respectful discussion about the Scriptures, while on the other hand, there were also those who (in some cases) became quite hostile when discussing doctrine. Of them all, there was one conversation that stands out in my memory; it was with a couple who seemed to be fairly representative of many others in the church. Both the husband and the wife had heard a great deal about me and about my convictions before I had arrived. In fact they had received, from a number of members, some dainty morsels of insight about what I *probably* would do if I became their pastor; however, most of these conjectures were untrue and were remarkably negative. Those who spoke to this couple about me used very familiar labels when describing me. As I spoke with this couple, it became apparent to me that they had been heavily influenced with rumors, innuendos, and labels. Because of this, the wife became particularly anxious, and even visibly angry, when she asked me: "Are you a Calvinist? Do you believe in limited atonement?" Questions such as these are typically conversational *ice makers* rather than *ice breakers!* But as the Savior often did when being queried in this fashion,[1] I asked her to explain what she meant by the very labels that she used. This surprised her. Because of my question, she found herself in the awkward position of having to explain what she meant by what she said. With much difficulty she offered an answer, but with obvious

---

[1] Matthew 9:4, 14:31, 16:8, Mark 2:8, 10:18, 12:15-17; John 5:5-6, 18:23.

uncertainty. As I listened to her, it became clear to me that she didn't fully understand what those labels represented, either biblically or historically. All that she had heard from others was that Christians who believe in "xyz" are wrong and those who believe in "abc" are right; period - *end of discussion*! Her question to me was like many others that I have had throughout my ministry; it wasn't a question regarding Scripture, rather, it was a question that was merely hatched out of contention and misunderstanding based upon various traditions of men, rumors, clichés, stereotypes and *labels*. By now, the woman's excited demeanor drew a small crowd of people around us. But what happened next was particularly disarming: instead of engaging in discussions based upon church history, or theological labels, we did something that is too infrequent in the modern church - *we opened our Bibles*. I had them turn with me to a passage of Scripture where we explored just how *vast and victorious Christ's atoning work is*, and how central this truth will be in Heaven when all the saints of God will declare Christ's worth and glory. It was a memorable, but strange experience; for a brief moment in time, a man and his wife were being presented, not with the traditions of men, but with what God has said about the subject of the atonement. As I read these texts of Scripture, some of the bystanders drew closer. There were some onlookers whose countenances began to glow with a smile as the Scriptures were read, while others with stern expressions stood with obvious skepticism. At first, the couple seemed hesitant as we read the Scriptures, but they began to be calmed by the presentation of God's Word alone, rather than a man's opinions. I doubt that anyone had ever suggested to this couple that they read the very text that we examined in order to address the subject of the atonement. In some ways this text seemed to disarm them as they drew comfort from the truth of Christ's glorious victory of the cross. Though this respite had a pleasing sense to it at the moment, it was unfortunately short lived. Whatever joy this couple gleaned from the Scriptures soon withered away within a few weeks. Those bystanders and counselors who prepped this couple in the first place, had successfully debriefed them back to the "real" issues at hand; that is, rumors, labels, clichés - *the traditions of men*. It saddens my heart to say that this is not an uncommon experience for many in today's church; and for those who dare to bring forth the Scriptures in such a bitter environment, opposition and even hostility will not be uncommon.

Sadly, the church in America has created a new body of "truth" that has little to do with what the Bible says, but has a great deal to do with tradition. But instead of embracing manmade tradition, we must all go to God's Word *alone* for truth. The historic example of the Pharisees should fill our hearts with dread, knowing that we all have within us a great propensity to embrace the traditions of men, thinking that they provide some authority and help. It is no wonder that when their movement began, the Pharisees [*peruśiym – separatists*][2] sought to protect the law of God through their own teachings and *orally preserved creeds,*[3] but over time, these oral instructions became the revered traditions which were seen as essential for one's own life and spirituality. Despite their better intentions when they began, the Pharisees' legacy became one of deception and death; and at the root of their error was that ancient deception which rejects the absolute authority of God and His Word. In the end, such weeds of rebellion can stem from the thorns of legalism or, for that matter, from the rocky soils of liberalism, as is illustrated by Harry Emerson Fosdick:

---

[2] The Pharisees viewed themselves as being those who were the sole defenders of the Scriptures; thus they sought to *separate* themselves from all liberal influences.

[3] Emil Schürer <u>A History of the Jewish People in the Time of Christ</u> (Hendrickson Publishers), 2nd Division, Vol II, pp. 10-11.

"My conclusion was plain... I did not have to believe anything simply because it was in the Bible. The old basis of authority was gone. Truth was an open field to be explained. Nothing could be settled by a text."[4]

I mention Fosdick here as my *only example from church history*, since no Evangelical would lay claim to his liberal views on the atonement - *or his views on much of anything else for that matter*. Fosdick believed that he was free to explore truth *outside the pale of God's Holy Writ* and therefore his example reminds us that *liberalism, and legalism,* both flourish in the same useless soils of *human wisdom*. In Mr. Fosdick's case, he erred in his thinking because he rejected the truth that *everything is settled by the text of Scripture* rather than by the opinions or laws of men.[5] The point is simply this: God's Word is the only definitive and *final standard* regarding any dispute or question in life. Failure to understand *and apply* this crucial point leaves the body of Christ open to a whole host of errors which transcend human imagination. Thus, the body of Christ must not be drawn away by those who would snatch, ensnare, and choke out the Word of God as soon as it is preached.[6] Unfortunately, there is a rising population of those who are trying to settle the disputes of doctrine with something other than the text of Scripture, but this must be avoided at all costs. It is with this important conviction that I say to you that if anything is to be settled in this book, concerning the doctrine of Christ's victorious atonement, then let it be by God's Word, and God's Word alone; not by emotional story telling; not by man-made reason and logic; not by trying to find a middle ground between truth *and error*; not by traditions, clichés, rumors, or straw-man arguments; nor by

---

[4] Harry Emerson Fosdick, The Living of These Days (Harper & Brothers, New York), p. 52.
[5] John 17:17, Psalm 119:92.
[6] Matthew 13:19.

slandering Evangelical theologians from church history. Instead, let all matters be settled by the precious waters of Holy Writ. As the bride of Christ, we are to be cleansed and purified by nothing else.

Why "Victorious" Atonement
*Yet in all these things we are more than conquerors
through Him who loved us.*
Romans 8:37

I strongly believe in using those words which the Scriptures use and emphasize. I call this *thinking inside the Book*, that is, the Bible. Such an approach may not be cute, clever, or quippy, but at least it will be faithful to the Scriptures. Which then leads us to a very relevant question: why use the expression - *victorious atonement?* Well, for one very simple reason: it is *biblical.* For example, as seen in the above text (Romans 8:37), Paul teaches us that as believers we are *more than conquerors* because of Christ. His statement is founded upon the central reality of the Savior's victory since it was Christ who *conquered all through His work on the cross.*[7] This word *conqueror*, as it is translated, comes from the Greek word *nikaō*, which simply means *to be victorious.*[8] This word is variously used in the New Testament to describe Christ's overall dominion and authority which was established through the cross at Calvary. Matthew used this word in his Gospel, depicting the Lord's

---

[7] Romans 8:3 For what the law could not do in that it was weak through the flesh, God did by sending His own Son in the likeness of sinful flesh, on account of sin: He condemned sin in the flesh.

[8] G. *nikaō;* The word group denotes "victory" or "superiority," whether in the physical, legal or metaphorical sense, whether in mortal conflict or peaceful competition. Theological dictionary of the New Testament. 1964-c1976. Vols. 5-9 edited by Gerhard Friedrich. Vol. 10 compiled by Ronald Pitkin. (G. Kittel, G. W. Bromiley & G. Friedrich, Ed.) (electronic ed.) (Vol. 4, Page 942). Grand Rapids, MI: Eerdmans.

fulfillment of Isaiah 42, stating that Christ will *bring justice to victory*.[9] Paul used it in 1 Corinthians 15 to speak of Christ's triumphant death and resurrection when he said that God gives us *victory through our Lord Jesus Christ*. And the Lord taught His disciples to take courage because *He had overcome [nenikēka][10] the world*.[11] All of these biblical texts, which herald Christ's victory, are indeed precious and crucial; however there is one section of Scripture that presents a compelling and climactic vision of Christ as the Conqueror over all, and it is found in a book that some might least suspect – *the book of Revelation*. Allow me to explain further: In recent years, I had the great privilege of preaching through John's Apocalypse, during which time I discovered many important gems concerning Christ's victory as the Lamb of God. What a joyful and refreshing study it was, even though at times it brought fear and trepidation to my heart. I say fear and trepidation, because the book of Revelation represents *the whole Bible*, since it is the very encapsulation and completion of all redemptive history. It is also chock-full of unspeakable visions of the future reign of Christ with His people; visions and images which should cause any careful exegete to tremble with reverence and awe. But the experience of Revelation was, ultimately, one of abundant joy and blessing because this capstone of the Bible has a particular focus and

---

[9] Matthew 12:20-21 20 "A battered reed He will not break off, And a smoldering wick He will not put out, Until He leads justice to victory. 21 "And in His name the Gentiles will hope."

[10] Christ's use of the perfect active indicative here in John chapter 16 reminds us of the certainty of God's decree. The victory of the cross was still a future event to take place (in time) and yet by God's decree, Christ was already the *victorious Lamb of God* who was slain from before the foundation of the world (Revelation 13:8).

[11] John 16:33 "These things I have spoken to you, that in Me you may have peace. In the world you will have tribulation; but be of good cheer, I have overcome the world."

agenda: *to reveal the victorious reign of Jesus Christ, the Lamb of God, over all the nations.* For two and a half years our flock joined together and listened, with great anticipation, to the Apostle John's spectacular descriptions of what he saw in the prophetic visions given to him while on the isle of Patmos. Week after week we were able to affirm the great promise concerning the blessing that comes to those who hear and those who read the words of this prophecy:

> *Revelation 1:1-3: 1 The Revelation of Jesus Christ, which God gave Him to show to His bond-servants, the things which must shortly take place; and He sent and communicated it by His angel to His bond-servant John, 2 who bore witness to the word of God and to the testimony of Jesus Christ, even to all that he saw. 3 Blessed is he who reads and those who hear the words of the prophecy, and heed the things which are written in it; for the time is near.*

John's promise of blessing is certainly true, however I must confess that prior to this enriching experience, I had practically avoided this *Revelation of Jesus Christ* because I had often witnessed an abundance of eschatological controversy that has been stirred in the name of this important book. In my past experiences in church, the book of Revelation was typically treated more like an interesting puzzle, filled with clues and secrets that were to be deciphered in order to understand *the timing* of the final events of human history. While the book of Revelation does address important matters of eschatology, it must be understood that it has a much higher design than that of an *end-times timetable*. The book of Revelation is, principally, *a Revelation or disclosure of Jesus Christ as the victorious and triumphant Lamb of God*. To miss this point would be a devastating error. Unfortunately, many people do try to find the blessings of Revelation by handling it as an eschatological Rubik's Cube, thus missing the central point of the book itself. But when we look intently at the *One* whom John heralds in his

Apocalypse, it is frankly impossible to miss the blessings that he promised to all. Even to the very end, we see the final effects of Christ's victorious atonement revealed in the 21st chapter where the Lord promised that in the New Jerusalem there will be no more crying, no more pain, no more death,[12] and no one who practices abomination shall ever enter into His kingdom, but only those whose names are written in the Lamb's book of life.[13] And how can we be sure that all this will take place? Because we know that the Lord's promises are sure and that *He will accomplish all His sovereign will!* This vision of the victorious Lamb of God is crucial for the life and vitality of the church. Without it, we will suffer greatly and may even sink into the depths of momentary despair, as did the Apostle John in Revelation 5:

> *Revelation 5:1-4: And I saw in the right hand of Him who sat on the throne a scroll written inside and on the back, sealed with seven seals. 2 Then I saw a strong angel proclaiming with a loud voice, "Who is worthy to open the scroll and to loose its seals?" 3 And no one in heaven or on the earth or under the earth was able to open the scroll, or to look at it. 4 So I wept much, because no one was found worthy to open and read the scroll, or to look at it. [NKJV]*

If Revelation chapter 5 is anything, it is a chapter of great contrasts. The latter portion of the chapter is filled with exuberant praise and joy, however the first half is filled with weeping and great sorrow on the part of John. John wept *much* because no one was found worthy to open the scroll. As we see in the remainder of Revelation, the seals of this scroll represent God's final judgment, and with it, the final redemption of those who are His; thus, this sealed document can be viewed as God's authority to bring about the *final judgment*

---

[12] Revelation 21:3-5.
[13] Revelation 21:24-27.

and *redemption* of mankind. Such a vision as this would have brought great hope and excitement to the heart of John. But because it appeared to John that no one was found worthy to unfold the scroll in order to bring about these final events - *he wept*. By his reactions it would seem that he had momentarily forgotten the Savior's declaration that He was the Victor over the whole world;[14] but John's sorrow only set the stage for this announcement concerning Christ's *powerful victory*:

> *Revelation 5:5 But one of the elders said to me, "Do not cry! The Lion from the tribe of Judah, David's descendant, has won the victory [enikēsen][15] so that He is able to open the scroll and its seven seals." [NCV]*

It is amazing to consider that the for three years the Apostle John heard Christ with his own ears, saw Him with his own eyes, handled Him with his own hands,[16] and even witnessed His glorious resurrection; and yet *he had momentarily lost sight of Christ's nature as the triumphant Victor*. But when John was restored to this precious vision of Christ, *his sorrow was turned to great joy and praise*, as he beheld the host of heaven praising the Lamb of God:

> *Revelation 5:9-10: 9 And they *sang a new song, saying, "Worthy art Thou to take the book, and to break its seals; for Thou wast slain, and didst purchase for God with Thy blood men from every tribe and tongue and people and nation. 10 "And Thou hast made them to be a kingdom and priests to our God; and they will reign upon the earth."*

---

[14] John 16:33.
[15] The New Century Version (NCV) appropriately captures the aorist active indicative of *nikoō* with the translation: "won the victory."
[16] 1 John 1:1

Christ was *victorious* because He *purchased for God a great host of men throughout the earth*. Here indeed is the message of *victorious atonement!* It was this important message that quickly turned John from despair to delight. I am convinced that this is the very vision of Christ that the church must reclaim. The modern, despairing church desperately needs this life giving message of the atonement of Jesus Christ, for it is the very heart of the Gospel itself. She needs it for her personal holiness, sanctification, and true joy; she needs it in order to grow and develop in her worship and adoration of her Savior; she needs the message of the cross for the sake of God's institution of marriage and family, and she must herald Christ's victorious atonement in order to seek, passionately, the lost with the Gospel. Without this important doctrine, Christ's sheep will become spiritually malnourished, emaciated, weak, and filled with despair. Thus, it is very sad when the many benefits of this doctrine are hid in the cupboards of contention. Through many internal battles in the church, the biblical vision of Christ's victory is often clouded and even lost. The end result is that many in the church are weakened, disoriented, and distracted; many are busy fighting battles *that offer no real victories for anyone,* thus, a great number in the church today are just like John as he wept in despair. With this in mind, the church of Jesus Christ must understand that she has a great need to meditate on the Savior's certain victory through His sacrifice on the cross.

As the sheep of His pasture, it is our great joy to herald the glorious victory of our Good Shepherd![17]

---

[17] Psalm 100:3 Know that the Lord, He is God; It is He who has made us, and not we ourselves; We are His people and the sheep of His pasture.

An Agenda of Adoration

"Worthy are You to take the book and to break its seals; for You were slain, and purchased for God with Your blood men from every tribe and tongue and people and nation."
Revelation 5:9

The purpose of this book is quite simple: to give glory to God our Savior and thus foster a greater love among the children of God for the One who purchased our pardon – the Lamb of God, Jesus Christ. The means to this very important end will consist of delving into the joyful celebration of Christ's victorious work of atonement. To do this, we will look at many passages in Scripture; however, the celebratory praise of Revelation 5 will serve as the rudder for our overall journey. The value of Revelation chapter 5 should be clear, for it defines the Christian's true destination: *victorious worship*. This song of the Lamb is one which celebrates the perfect obedience of Jesus Christ through His sacrifice on the cross. It ratifies the fulfillment of many Old Testament and New Testament prophecies, and it reminds us that all that has been decreed by the eternal counsel of God *will be fulfilled with perfection*:

> Isaiah 46:9-10: 9 Remember the former things long past, For I am God, and there is no other; I am God, and there is no one like Me, 10 Declaring the end from the beginning And from ancient times things which have not been done, Saying, "My purpose will be established, And I will accomplish all My good pleasure."

Here is a victorious message indeed: Jesus Christ, the Lamb of God fulfilled the *good* pleasure of the Father by shedding His own blood and making an incomprehensibly vast purchase of men *out of every tribe, tongue, people, and nation*! All that the Lord has said He would accomplish, through the cross, will be accomplished with perfection. This song of the Lamb therefore draws us to great hope, joyful celebration, and profound worship. By contrast, we must affirm that the song of the Lamb is not a hymn of lament, nor is it a dirge. It does not bemoan some perceived "failure" in God's eternal decree of the cross, for there is no failure in the outworking of God's good and perfect will – *He will accomplish all His good pleasure*. It does not leave us weeping like John did as he momentarily forgot Christ's victory as the Savior. No, the song of the Lamb lifts us beyond our vain human speculations and transports us to the truth of Christ's triumph. Therefore, like the Apostle John, we have a great and continual need to behold the Lamb, and His victory through the cross, so that our lives and ministries may be characterized by *joyful service* rather than *sorrow and despair*. This then is the clear, unabashed agenda of this book: *to draw the reader to this needful meditation on Christ's victorious atonement.* Someday, we will be in glory with Him and we will see Him as He is. There and then, we will all sing the song of victory: the song of the Lamb.[18] But until then, let us come to the throne of His grace and ask the Lord to prepare us for that eternal chorale. In some way you can consider your time spent in this book to be a form of heavenly choir rehearsal, designed to prepare us all for that day when we will declare the worthiness of the Lamb to receive "*all power and riches and wisdom and might and honor and glory and blessing... and dominion forever and ever, amen*" *(Revelation 5:12-14).* So warm your voices; open your Bibles and let the choir practice begin as we behold the victorious Lamb of God, who was slain before the foundation of the world.[19]

---

[18] Revelation 7:9-10, 15:1-4.
[19] Revelation 13:8.

ALL NATIONS UNDER GOD

CHRIST'S VICTORIOUS ATONEMENT

DEFINED

For Whom Did Christ Die?

For I have come down from heaven, not to do My own will, but the will of Him who sent Me. This is the will of Him who sent Me, that of all that He has given Me I lose nothing, but raise it up on the last day.
John 6:38-39

By introducing the greatest story ever told, I have thus presented to you *its important message,* as well as *my reason for using the expression: victorious atonement.* Now we need to address the important matter of *defining* Christ's victorious atonement by the Scriptures alone. In particular, we need to search out *what was won* when Christ gave His life as an atonement for sin. Now at this point in our discussion, it is typically the case that people will raise that familiar question regarding the *intent of the atonement:* "For whom did Christ die?" In fact, it almost seems like standard procedure to do so. When searching out the question of the atonement's *intent* [the purpose of the atonement] or the *extent* [the actual effect of it], it is typical for conversations to gravitate towards a binary discussion dominated by two words: *limited and unlimited.* The answer normally sought in such investigations has to do with whether Christ died for all men *without exception* (unlimited) or for all the elect in Christ throughout the world (limited). This information is then thought to satisfy the questions regarding the *intent* and *extent* of the atonement. In some sense the Christian culture has been programmed to think of the atonement in terms of its *redemptive intent* and *extent* only. Therefore the "whom" in the aforementioned question is typically thought of as being those sinners *for whom* Christ died. Christian literature, sermons, hymns, and songs typically make this the immediate focus. There was even that popular song by David Meece which sought to answer the question before us, entitled - "We were the Reason":

Christ's Victorious Atonement Defined

And we were the reason that He gave His life
We were the reason that He suffered and died
To a world that was lost He gave all He could give
To show us the reason to live[20]

We were the reason, as the song says. The particular emphasis of this song is clearly focused upon Christ's gift of salvation given *to sinners*, and suppositions that the *principal intent* of the atonement was the salvation of mankind. While there are several wonderful truths in this song, it should be noted that there is an important difference of emphasis given to us in the *infallible* song of the Lamb:

Revelation 5:9: And they sang a new song, saying, "Worthy are You to take the book and to break its seals; for You were slain, and purchased for God with Your blood men from every tribe and tongue and people and nation.

Yes, *we* were victoriously purchased by the Lamb's shed blood, however, we were ultimately redeemed *for God*. We must not underestimate this little prepositional phrase - *for God*, for it informs us that our redemption serves an *intention* of God that is much higher than ourselves. This ultimate *intention* of God's will is His own glory and good pleasure.[21] Unfortunately, this biblical observation is rarely unfolded before the heated debates regarding the atonement's *intent* or *extent*, and this is no small problem. To illustrate this point, let us consider a similar error committed in John chapter 12. It is here that we are told that Jesus was reclining

---

[20] David Meece and Dwight Liles, *We Are The Reason*, There I Go Again, 2002.
[21] "Sinners are purchased *for God*. Redemption is not aimless; they are bought so that they may belong to God (cf. 1 Cor. 6:19-20)." Leon Morris, <u>Revelation</u>, Tyndale New Testament Commentaries (William B. Eerdmans Publishing Company, Grand Rapids, Michigan), p. 97.

at a table for a feast in Bethany where He was with Lazarus, Martha, Mary, and the twelve. At this feast, Mary did something wonderful: she took a pound of *very costly perfume* and spent it entirely by anointing the feet of the Lord, using her own hair to do so. The house was being filled with the fragrance of the perfume as the disciples complained about its waste;[22] but Christ used this moment to teach everyone something concerning the beauty of what Mary had done: Mary's *act of giving* was far more fragrant than the perfume itself, because she *loved and cherished Christ above all*.[23] Unfortunately, the disciples had focused on Mary's gift, *rather than the surpassing value of Christ*. Too often has the church entered into this error by failing to focus on the ultimate beauty of Christ and His work on the cross. Illustratively speaking, we must recognize that while the church has been made fragrant by the Lord's atoning sacrifice,[24] we must never lose sight of the greater purpose for which we have been redeemed in the first place - *that we would be lovingly presented as Christ's aromatic gift to the Father*.

> *1 Corinthians 15:28 Now when all things are made subject to Him, then the Son Himself will also be subject to Him who put all things under Him, that God may be all in all. [NKJV]*

Christ's death, burial, and resurrection serve this consummate purpose: that all things subjected to God the Son, will be subjected to God the Father, in glory - *that God may be all in all*. Thus, the victory of the cross is a victory that is from God, and *for God Himself!* By this we can clearly see that the work of Christ on the

---

[22] See Matthew 28:8 for a fuller description of the disciples' response.

[23] Matthew 26:13 "Truly I say to you, wherever this gospel is preached in the whole world, what this woman has done shall also be spoken of in memory of her."

[24] Ephesians 5:2 ... Christ ... gave Himself up for us, an offering and a sacrifice to God as a fragrant aroma.

cross was a God-centered work and not a man-centered one. This truth affirms the centrality of God in all that He wills and does:

Romans 11:36 For of Him and through Him and to Him are all things, to whom be glory forever. Amen.

All things are from Him (John 1:2-3); all things are mediated through His sovereign Providence (Isaiah 45:5-7); and all things are ultimately for His glory (John 12:28). By this we must understand that the redeemed of God are just a part of a much larger purpose: *the glory and good pleasure of God Himself*.[25] In light of this I would suggest that it would be better to say that we are <u>a</u> *reason* that He gave His life. Christ's sheep are a very important reason to be sure, but they are not *the reason* to the exclusion of a much greater purpose. Therefore, we again ask: "For whom did Christ die?" or "What was the highest intent found in the sacrifice of Christ?" Answer: *He sacrificed Himself, principally, for His Father in Heaven*. When we view the subject of the atonement in this important light, crucial truths begin to crystallize for us. By this we can gain greater clarity concerning the common queries regarding the *intent* and *extent* of Christ's atonement. In fact, whatever one might be tempted to say about either (*intent or extent*), there is only one biblical conclusion that all must draw lest they be guilty of great error: *Christ's sacrifice on the cross bore no failure, but was an immutable victory accomplished by the Son, for the Father*. The Lamb of God was entirely successful, both in the intent and extent of His atoning sacrifice! To suggest anything else is a dangerous matter for it defiles our understanding of the nature of the Son and of the Father. Therefore, in this chapter we will examine the crucial questions regarding the atonement in order to render a full

---

[25] John Owen, The Death of Death in the Death of Christ, *The Works of John Owen* (Banner of Truth Trust, Carlisle, Pennsylvania), pp. 200-203.

definition of *Christ's victorious atonement*. To do this, we will examine the atonement's *intent, immutability* and *extent*.

The Intent of Christ's Atonement
(A Victory Of Eternal Love)

*Therefore My Father loves Me, because I lay down My life
that I may take it again.*
John 10:17

God's love for mankind is a sweet and cherished truth that is wonderfully repeated in the Scriptures. Like a moth to a flame, we are quickly drawn to these texts because we thrive on the truth that our Heavenly Father loves us. Like little children, the Lord's bosom of infinite love calms our every fear and distress as soon as we rest our heads on Him. That God would choose to love those who were unlovely is such an incomprehensible truth that it boggles the mind, and yet we know that while we were yet sinners, *Christ died for us.*[26] And yet an exclusive focus on this *one aspect* of God's love could leave us detached from a greater love relationship that existed long before we were born, or the heavens and the earth were ever made. This love relationship is an unspeakably intimate, deep, perfect, and holy one which has existed for all eternity:

> *John 17:24 Father, I desire that they also whom You gave Me may be with Me where I am, that they may behold My glory which You have given Me; for You loved Me before the foundation of the world.*

What a wonderful glimpse of Trinitarian love this is! Before any descendent of Adam was ever the object of God's love, the Son was the *Beloved One* of the Father, from all eternity. This observation is profoundly important, for I find that discussions regarding the

---

[26] Romans 5:8 But God demonstrates His own love toward us, in that while we were yet sinners, Christ died for us.

inter-Trinitarian relationship are often neglected or misunderstood. There is even, I believe, a common tendency to reduce the relationship of the Father, Son, and Holy Spirit to a *merely functional one*. Especially when we try to comprehend God's immutability, we may be tempted to think of the Lord as being a motionless being. But the fact that God is immutable, and therefore does not change,[27] does not mean that one should think of Him as a lifeless statue. The living God is a relationally loving God. This has been true in all eternity past, and it will be true forever without end. And this essential attribute of love has always found perfect expression within the Trinity; even before the creation of the angels and mankind. You see, long before the foundation of the world, the Father loved the Son, and with perfect reciprocity, the Son has always loved the Father:

> *John 1:1,18 In the beginning was the Word, and the Word was with God, and the Word was God...18 No one has seen God at any time. The only begotten Son, who is in the bosom of the Father, He has declared Him.*

John gives us two expressions, in the first chapter of his Gospel, that help us to understand better the nature of the relationship between the Father and the Son. First, John says that the Son was *with* God. This brief statement is in no way insignificant, especially in view of John's use of the preposition *pros* rather than *para* or *meta*. While context ultimately determines the use of these words, these latter prepositions [*para* and *meta*] tend to represent a more *general form of association*. But *pros* normally means *towards*, which represents a more intense notion of proximity or relationship. For example, you could be sitting *with* or *beside*

---

[27] Malachi 3:6 "For I am the Lord, I do not change; Therefore you are not consumed, O sons of Jacob."

someone at a restaurant and perhaps never talk to them, especially if your back is to them. However, in an intimate dinner with a loved one, you are positioned *towards them*, even face to face in private discourse. This is the picture that John gives us, as William Hendriksen affirms:

> And the Word was face to face with God (*pros ton theon*). The meaning is that the Word existed in the closest possible fellowship with the father, and that he took supreme delight in this communion.[28]

The Son of God was not casually with the Father, but He was *intimately towards* the Father in a personal and eternal love relationship.[29] John's second description of the Son's relationship with the Father comes in verse 18 of the same chapter, where he describes the only Begotten Son as being *in the bosom of the Father*. For the Apostle of love this imagery was very personal to him, for at the last supper of Christ it was he who was reclining in the *Savior's bosom*. In both cases, this is the unmistakable image of familial love. As a picture of the Son's love for the Father, it shows us that His love abounds with an eternal affection and esteem. The myriads of myriads and thousands of thousands of angels could never, in all eternity, tabulate the extent of the Father's love for the Son, nor the Son for the Father. So how important is this message of Trinitarian love to our world today? What relevance might this have to this generation, or any generation for that matter? Plenty:

---

[28] William Hendriksen, New Testament Commentary, The Gospel of John (Baker Book House, Grand Rapids, Michigan), p. 70.

[29] John 17:24 "Father, I desire that they also, whom Thou hast given Me, be with Me where I am, in order that they may behold My glory, which Thou hast given Me; for Thou didst love Me before the foundation of the world."

John 14:31 ...the world must learn that I love the Father and that I do exactly what my Father has commanded me. Come now; let us leave. [NIV]

The Son's love for the Father was so important *that He wanted the whole world to know it*! Consider the context of this important passage for a moment: this expression of Christ's love for the Father stands between His betrayal by Judas (John 13) and His coming crucifixion (John 19). Therefore, when He said to His remaining disciples "come now; let us leave" He was inviting them to proceed with Him towards Gethsemane where He would be arrested, and subsequently crucified at Golgotha. But before they were to proceed on this journey towards His own death, He wanted them to understand this crucial truth: what He was about to do, He would do out of a *great love for the Father* (John 14:31). This is indeed a compelling thought. When we think of the worldwide message of the Gospel, we most often think of Christ's love *for mankind*. But we must also comprehend that the other worldwide message that Christ desires to be spread abroad is *His love for the Father which led Him to the cross*. But these are not separate messages; rather they are indelibly linked as one. You see, the Son, who laid down His life for His sheep, did so as an act of *loving obedience to the Father*. This is why Christ declared that His worldwide message was twofold: 1. "I love the Father" and 2. "I do exactly what my Father commanded me." Thus, when Christ died for our sins, He did so out of His tender affections for the Father:

John 6:38-39: 38 For I have come down from heaven, not to do My own will, but the will of Him who sent Me. 39 And this is the will of Him who sent Me, that of all that He has given Me I lose nothing, but raise it up on the last day.

Christ's obedience to the Father was not a mere mechanism consisting of duty alone; rather His obedience was infinitely embedded in the eternal love relationship between the Father and the Son. This precious truth is what the Son of God wanted the world to know. And the Son's love for the Father, which led Him to that cross, was reciprocated by the Father who loved Him dearly in view of His loving and immutable obedience:

> *John 10:17 For this reason the Father loves Me, because I lay down My life that I may take it again.*

Here is the highest victory of the cross – the victory of God's love: the love of the Father for the Son and of the Son for the Father. Should we miss this principle, we would be guilty of walking past a vast ocean of God-glorifying truth, for without the loving, perfect, and holy obedience of Jesus Christ there would be no atonement *for anyone*. What God required of His Son was absolute justice and perfection, thus out of His great love for the Father, the Son fulfilled all:

> *Isaiah 53:11 ...By His knowledge My righteous Servant shall justify many, For He shall bear their iniquities.*

Jesus Christ, the Lamb of God, was the Father's *righteous Servant* from the beginning of His incarnation to His righteous sacrifice on the cross. Therefore, nothing that the Savior ever did, said, or thought could ever be associated with sin or rebellion; therefore every aspect of His life confirmed that He was *unblemished* and *undefiled*.[30] As a man He was surrounded with the temptations

---

[30] 1 Peter 1:18-19 18 knowing that you were not redeemed with corruptible things, like silver or gold, from your aimless conduct received by tradition from your fathers,19 but with the precious blood of Christ, as of a lamb without blemish and without spot. [NKJV].

which fill our world, yet He was without sin.[31] And though He suffered great hostility by sinners against Himself, He remained just until the end - *always looking to please the Father*:

> *John 8:29 And He who sent Me is with Me. The Father has not left Me alone, for I always do those things that please Him.*

The life that He lived was entirely offered up, in love, for the good pleasure of His Father. And the death that He died was an unblemished sacrifice offered up with no less devotion:

> *Hebrews 9:14 how much more shall the blood of Christ, who through the eternal Spirit offered Himself without spot to God, cleanse your conscience from dead works to serve the living God?*

The holy Lamb of God remained unblemished until the very end and thus He offered up Himself as a perfect sacrifice to God. It is this sacrifice of Christ's that has rendered the satisfaction of God's justice, *so that God is both just and the justifier of the one who has faith in Jesus.*[32]

What a great and eternal victory is the cross of Jesus Christ!

Our holy and victorious Savior, out of a great love for the Father, *always did the things that were pleasing to Him.* If it were not for Christ's holiness and unfailing obedience to the Father, *there would be no atonement at all!* Without the immutable, Trinitarian love of God there would be no cross, no redemption – no hope for the world whatsoever. But because of His loving and immutable

---

[31] Hebrews 2:18 For in that He Himself has suffered, being tempted, He is able to aid those who are tempted.
[32] Romans 3:21-26.

obedience to the Father's will Christ has rendered this certain result: *a great multitude throughout the earth, which no one can count,* will taste the goodness of the Lord through the redemption that is in the Lamb of God. Here is a secure anchor for our discussion of the atonement. Whatever one might want to say about Christ's sacrifice, it is an unavoidable truth, *a truth worthy of world renown - the Son loved the Father and pleased Him through the gift of the many that were redeemed by His unblemished sacrifice.* Here is the *principal intent* of the cross of the Lamb of God!

THE IMMUTABILITY OF CHRIST'S ATONEMENT
(A VICTORY OF ABSOLUTE PERFECTION)

The Lord of hosts has sworn saying, "Surely, just as I
have intended so it has happened,
and just as I have planned
so it will stand..."
Isaiah 14:24

What God intends and plans – *will stand.* Isaiah 14:24 teaches us, very clearly, that there is a direct relationship between God's will and His works; all that He *determines* to do, *will be done - immutably.* It is this foundational truth which reminds us that God is faithful and true without any variation or shifting shadow;[33] therefore, He is trustworthy in every way. Similarly, we must remember that there are two things that the Lord has said He *cannot do,* under any circumstance: He *cannot lie,*[34] nor can He *sin.*[35] Of course, the former act would ultimately lead to the latter

---

[33] James 1:17 Every good gift and every perfect gift is from above, and comes down from the Father of lights, with whom there is no variation or shadow of turning. [NKJV]

[34] Hebrews 6:17-18.

[35] James 1:13-15.

since *it is a sin to lie*.³⁶ This important truth, regarding God's immutable holiness, must not be seen as mere decoration on a theologian's chalkboard; instead, it is a truth that is central to our understanding of the Lord's nature as being trustworthy in all His promises. It is this foundation that establishes the surety of any Christian, for in His promises we have an anchor for the soul:

> *Hebrews 6:17-20: 17 In the same way God, desiring even more to show to the heirs of the promise the unchangeableness of His purpose, interposed with an oath, 18 in order that by two unchangeable things, in which it is impossible for God to lie, we may have strong encouragement, we who have fled for refuge in laying hold of the hope set before us. 19 This hope we have as an anchor of the soul, a hope both sure and steadfast and one which enters within the veil, 20 where Jesus has entered as a forerunner for us, having become a high priest forever according to the order of Melchizedek.*

The believer can know for certain that God's *promises* and His *oaths* are immutable, *because it is impossible for God to lie*. This crucial truth is what the author of Hebrews calls *an anchor of the soul* for every child of God. This message was crucial for the recipients of this epistle, especially in light of the great afflictions and hostilities that they faced in the world.³⁷ Their hope had been fading,³⁸ therefore, this letter was sent to them so that their confidence in God's promises would be regained. What was important for them in their day is equally needful for the modern church! Though the trials visiting the American church have little to do with the forms of tribulation mentioned in Hebrews, we must still understand that today's church faces a most serious threat

---

[36] Leviticus 19:11, Ephesians 4:25.
[37] Hebrews 10:32 But recall the former days in which, after you were illuminated, you endured a great struggle with sufferings:
[38] Hebrews 12:3.

from within. By disproportionally battling over just one aspect of Christ's atonement, there are many today who, whether haplessly or knowingly, are challenging this bedrock principle concerning the immutability of God's oaths and promises. But whatever one might say about the many attributes of God, *let no one ever conclude that God is a liar*! A deity whose *oaths and promises are mutable* is an idol at best. But the Almighty God, whose powerful Word was the instrument of all creation, can be trusted in all His *oaths* and *promises* – Always! Much more will be said concerning the importance of this message of hope via God's promises in the next chapter, but for now we must consider the implications of God's immutable promises in relationship to the atonement. Simply put – what the Lord says He will do, will be done without flaw or imperfection. More particularly, what the Lord says He will do *can be viewed concurrently as a completed work* for there is no distinction in the unchangeableness of His *decrees* and *acts*.[39] This is why the Lamb of God's sacrifice is spoken of as being accomplished historically, from before the foundation of the world:

Revelation 13:8: All who dwell on the earth will worship him, whose names have not been written in the Book of Life of the Lamb slain from the foundation of the world. [NKJV]

Those who will commit the debauchery of worshipping the antichrist will be the ones whose names *have not been written in the Book of Life of the Lamb slain from the foundation of the world*. In this important verse, John used the same verbal[40] to describe the Lamb's completed work as he did in Revelation 5:6, but this time he

---

[39] Isaiah 14:24.
[40] G. *esphagmenon* – Perfect passive participle [accusative case]. The perfect participle speaks of antecedent time and often serves [as in the above case] as a verbal adjective. Therefore the Lamb is adjectively described as the One who, in past time, was sacrificed.

advanced the historic thought further back to the *foundation of the world*.⁴¹ Therefore, this sacrifice of the Lamb of God was spoken of as an established reality before time began because the Lord's eternal decree made certain the reality of Christ's crucifixion. Such a decretive certainty of the cross is frequently affirmed in the Scriptures:

> ***As affirmed by the Apostle Peter: Acts 2:23*** *Him, being delivered by the determined purpose and foreknowledge of God, you have taken by lawless hands, have crucified, and put to death.* ***Acts 3:18*** *But those things which God foretold by the mouth of all His prophets, that the Christ would suffer, He has thus fulfilled.* ***1 Peter 1:18-20*** *... you were ... redeemed ... with the precious blood of Christ, as of a lamb without blemish and without spot. He indeed was foreordained before the foundation of the world, but was manifest in these last times for you.*
>
> ***As affirmed by the disciples in the presence of the Apostles John and Peter:*** *Acts 4:27-28: 27 For truly against Your holy Servant Jesus, whom You anointed, both Herod and Pontius Pilate, with the Gentiles and the people of Israel, were gathered together 28 to do whatever Your hand and Your purpose determined before to be done.*

The great number of texts which affirm this unfailing relationship between *God's promises* and *the certain outcome of those promises*, go well beyond the scope of this book; however, these four Christological texts remind us that the Lamb's atoning work on the cross is the chief gem in the crown of all of God's immutable

---

⁴¹ Without a doubt, the applicability of the perfect participle is obvious since Christ died on Calvary at a time in history. But John goes further and advances this historical thought to the ultimate point of history when he adds to the verbal adjective: "before the foundation of the world." At that point, John identified the *event of the cross* with God's *eternal decree of the cross*: the one *immutably led to the other*.

decrees.[42] How His sacrifice was made,[43] when it was made,[44] and why it was made[45] are the very issues which *stand securely* on the *oaths* and *promises* of God.

We can thank the Lord that His oaths and promises are *immutable*. If this were not true, then the world would be left with no redemptive hope. The importance of this point cannot be underestimated in light of our discussion concerning Christ's victorious atonement. It provides us with a sound basis of *reason* by which we can further understand and define the immutable victory of the cross. I say *reason* here because it is our duty to *reason* in only one particular way: *from the Scriptures*. This is the Apostolic model set before us in God's Word,[46] and it is the only safeguard that we have to keep us from the foolishness and frailties of our own human logic and reason. Consider God's decree of the cross for a moment. Just by looking at the relationship between God's *intent* of the cross (His predetermined purpose) and the resultant *effect* (the actual event of the cross), we see why Christ is called the Victor in God's Word:

> **Intent**[Rev. 13:8] ≫ **Effect**[Acts 2:23] = **His Victory of the Cross**

---

[42] Colossians 1:13-20.

[43] Acts 2:23, 3:18, 4:27-28.

[44] Romans 5:6 For when we were still without strength, in due time Christ died for the ungodly.

[45] John 12:31, Mark 10:45.

[46] Acts 17:2-3: 2 Then Paul, as his custom was, went in to them, and for three Sabbaths reasoned with them from the Scriptures, 3 explaining and demonstrating that the Christ had to suffer and rise again from the dead, and saying, "This Jesus whom I preach to you is the Christ."

Christ's sacrifice on the cross was a wonderful victory such that it established the complete fulfillment of the Father's loving desire and will. The cross of Jesus Christ was an immutable success in that it was an abundant expression of love from the Son to the Father,[47] and from the Father to the Son.[48] As well, it was a glorious victory such that God's oaths and promises were affirmed as being immutably true. Thus, the cross of Jesus Christ stands as the greatest triumph of *the Lord's immutable love and power* in all of human history.

THE EXTENT OF CHRIST'S ATONEMENT (A VICTORY OF ABUNDANT REDEMPTION)

I looked, and behold, a great multitude which no one could number, of all nations, tribes, peoples, and tongues, standing before the throne and before the Lamb
Revelation 7:9-10

The first victory of the atonement which we examined was that victory of love whereby Christ obeyed the Father and offered Himself to God as a sacrifice without blemish. This we identified as being the *principal intent* of the atonement, acknowledging that the work of the cross was a God-centered, not man-centered, event. We then considered the decree of the cross and, with it, its successful fulfillment, observing that the one immutably established the reality of the other. But we must now move to the question of the *atonement's extent*, remembering that Christ's atoning work is repeatedly called a victory, especially in the songs of praise to the Lamb in the book of Revelation. Considering the details of Revelation chapters 5 and 7, we can very simply say that the extent of Christ's atonement is *massive*. It effectually secured

---

[47] John 14:31.
[48] John 10:17.

the redemption of a great multitude which no human can number! No one needs a Math degree to deduce that this is a lot of people! Here then is the other significant victory of the cross. John's vision of the saints of God in Revelation 7:9-10 must have been absolutely overwhelming. John saw, not a few, but many in glory (beyond his ability to assess) because of the Lamb who was slain. This fantastic vision reflects the great song of the Lamb in Revelation 5:9, which we have already examined:

> *Revelation 5:9 And they *sang a new song, saying, "Worthy art Thou to take the book, and to break its seals; for Thou wast slain, and didst purchase for God with Thy blood men from every tribe and tongue and people and nation."*

Let me offer an additional observation from this important song: John described the abundant redemption of humanity as being that which will extend throughout the world. *Every*, says John, *tribe, tongue, people and nation* will be represented in glory because of the Lamb's shed blood. However, John does not say that *all men* from all tribes, tongues, peoples and nations will be the recipients of salvation. The extent of the Lamb's redemptive work is clarified when the Apostle speaks of men *from* (lit. *out of*),[49] *every* tribe, tongue, people and nation. This clarification eliminates any possible notions of universalism. It is not that every man will be saved, but *many* are his purchased ones. Therefore, in that day in glory we will see the fruit of Christ's atonement such that there will

---

[49] The expression *ek pasēs kai glōssēs kai laou kai ethnous* begins with the preposition *ek* in order to communicate the equivalent of an ablatival sense of separation, i.e., *some out of all nations* etc. This preposition (along with *apo*) came to replace the ablatival case, when used with the genitive "so much so that the ablatival concept is increasingly expressed with *apo* or *ek* rather than with the 'naked' genitive form." Daniel B. Wallace, <u>Greek Grammar Beyond the Basics</u>, (Zondervan Publishing House, Grand Rapids, Michigan), pp. 77-107.

be representatives *out of all* the earth, worshipping the Lamb of God. This is indeed an *extensive, vast, and abundant atonement!* One day this vast sea of humanity, from *all nations,* will be under the Savior's loving reign in glory. This disclosure concerning the *effect* of Christ's redeeming work is very significant, for it helps us to understand Scripture's emphasis on the extent of the atonement. Such an *extensive atonement* is consistently presented throughout the Bible and provides the very basis of hope concerning the Savior's coming victory. At the beginning of Revelation chapter 5 we saw that John wept because he had forgotten the fact that Christ was the Victor; this was partially due to the fact that he had lost sight of the many wonderful promises in the Old Testament that look forward to this immutable victory of Christ, as in the case of Zechariah chapter 9:

> *Zechariah 9:9-10: 9 Rejoice greatly, O daughter of Zion! Shout in triumph, O daughter of Jerusalem! Behold, your king is coming to you; He is just and endowed with salvation, Humble, and mounted on a donkey, even on a colt, the foal of a donkey. 10 And I will cut off the chariot from Ephraim, And the horse from Jerusalem; And the bow of war will be cut off. And He will speak peace to the nations; And His dominion will be from sea to sea, And from the River to the ends of the earth.*

Here is yet another prophecy which calls the reader out of despair unto great rejoicing because of the coming Redeemer. Clearly, Christ fulfilled this important prophecy in every way: the humble Lamb of God triumphantly entered Jerusalem as the King of kings, who in His justice could have condemned us all; but in His great love was endowed with salvation. That He was endowed with salvation means that He possessed a great bounty of grace and mercy for mankind! This expression, *endowed with salvation,* carries the idea of an abundant victory. In fact this phrase could be translated as *conqueror or victor*; i.e., *victorious with salvation*.[50] Such is the emphasis of the verbal used, and such is the overall context of the prophecy of Zechariah 9:9-10! This concept of Christ's great endowment of salvation continues into verse 10 when we see that the promised Savior will establish true peace and His kingdom will extend well beyond the borders of Israel - *from sea to sea and from the River to the ends of the earth*. This expression concerning the Lord's *extensive reign of peace* reflects John's vision of Christ's vast kingdom in Revelation. Here again we see the perfect relationship between the Lord's promises and His fulfillment of those promises:

Intent[(Zech. 9:9-10)] ≫ **Effect**[(Rev. 5:5-10)] = **Victorious Atonement**

The redemptive *intent* of God, as expressed in Zechariah 9:9-10, and the redemptive *effect*, as seen in Revelation 5:5-10, stand together as the immutable outworking of God's will. Here are the perfect *oaths* and *promises* of our God: what the Lord decreed to do, He did,[51] immutably, through the perfect obedience of the Beloved One.[52] This same hope of a vast, redemptive harvest is repeatedly affirmed in both the Old and the New Testaments:

- *Psalm 65:5 By awesome deeds You answer us in righteousness, O God of our salvation, You who are the trust of all the ends of the earth and of the farthest sea.*

---

[50] The niphal participial form of *yăš'ă* [*nûšă'*] can be rendered as *victor* or *conqueror*: "*nûšă'* conqueror, Zec. 9:9 [In this passage of course it refers to Christ as *bestowing salvation*]." Gesenius, W., & Tregelles, S. P. (2003). Gesenius' Hebrew and Chaldee lexicon to the Old Testament Scriptures. Bellingham, WA: Logos Research Systems, Inc., p. 374.

[51] Romans 8:3.

[52] Ephesians 1:5-6.

- *Psalm 67:1-2 God be gracious to us and bless us, and cause His face to shine upon us—[Selah]. 2 That Thy way may be known on the earth, Thy salvation among all nations.*

- *Isaiah 49:6 I will also make You a light of the nations So that My salvation may reach to the end of the earth.*

- *Isaiah 52:10 The Lord has bared His holy arm In the sight of all the nations, That all the ends of the earth may see The salvation of our God.*

- *Luke 2:30-32: 30 [Simeon-]... my eyes have seen Your salvation, 31 Which You have prepared in the presence of all peoples, 32 A Light of revelation to the Gentiles, And the glory of Your people Israel."*

- *John 6:51 "I am the living bread which came down from heaven. If anyone eats of this bread, he will live forever; and the bread that I shall give is My flesh, which I shall give for the life of the world."*

- *John 8:12 Then Jesus spoke to them again, saying, "I am the light of the world. He who follows Me shall not walk in darkness, but have the light of life."*

- *1 John 4:14 And we have seen and testify that the Father has sent the Son as Savior of the world.*

- *John 11:51-52: 51 [Caiaphas...] prophesied that Jesus was going to die for the nation, 52 and not for the nation only, but in order that He might also gather together into one the children of God who are scattered abroad.*

The Scriptures have always promised that the atoning work of Christ would extend well beyond the borders of Israel, reaching out to the remotest ends of the earth. This good pleasure of the Lord, which He has promised to fulfill, establishes the fact that, not only Israel, but *all the nations of the earth* will cumulatively yield a great harvest of souls in the last day. This is the same promise that was entrusted to Abraham the believer, who is called the father of all who believe:

> *Genesis 22:15-18: Then the angel of the* L̲ᴏʀᴅ *called to Abraham a second time from heaven, 16 and said, "By Myself I have sworn, declares the Lord, because you have done this thing and have not withheld your son, your only son, 17 indeed I will greatly bless you, and I will greatly multiply your seed as the stars of the heavens and as the sand which is on the seashore; and your seed shall possess the gate of their enemies. 18 "In your seed all the nations of the earth shall be blessed, because you have obeyed My voice."*

Here again we see the promise of God's extensive blessing being given to a great multitude throughout the earth. This important Old Testament promise is crucial, and is clearly explained for us by the Apostle Paul:

> *Galatians 3:7-9: 7 Therefore, be sure that it is those who are of faith who are sons of Abraham. 8 The Scripture, foreseeing that God would justify the Gentiles by faith, preached the gospel beforehand to Abraham, saying, "All the nations will be blessed in you." 9 So then those who are of faith are blessed with Abraham, the believer.*

This Gospel message which was preached to Abraham reminds us that those who trust the Savior are blessed with Abraham *the believer*.[53] These believing sons of Abraham will not be few in number, rather, there will be many drawn out of all the nations. Thus, it is in Christ alone that the blessing of Abraham will be

---

[53] Galatians 3:7-9, Romans 4:9-25.

extended to a vast number among the nations,[54] such that many will be there in final glory, just as the Son of Man promised in light of the victory of His atoning work:

Mark 10:45 For even the Son of Man did not come to be served, but to serve, and to give His life a ransom for many.

This precious promise of our Lord is very important. The surety of this promise is rooted in the loving and immutable obedience of the Son to the Father. What Christ set out to do out of love for the Father, *He did*, without a single element of imperfection. Therefore, the *many* who have been ransomed shall certainly dwell in the glory of Heaven, forever. In summary, here is the victory of Christ's atonement, in its *intent, immutability, and extent*:

- ***The Principal Intent of the Atonement (A Victory of Great Love):*** *The highest intent of the atonement lays a very important foundation for us: Christ's highest intention was rooted in His love for the Father, such that He would render Himself as a holy sacrifice to God. The Father looked upon His Beloved Son, and by that sacrifice, was satisfied and glorified. Christ purchased His people by His own blood so that they would be offered up to the Father as a gift of eternal love – so that God may by all in all (1 Corinthians 15:28). Here is the consummate victory of Trinitarian love.*

- ***The Immutability of the Atonement (A Work of Absolute Perfection):*** *The Lord's oaths and promises are trustworthy, because our Lord does not lie. Heaven and earth will pass away,*

---

[54] Galatians 3:14, 29: 14 in order that in Christ Jesus the blessing of Abraham might come to the Gentiles, so that we would receive the promise of the Spirit through faith ... 29 And if you belong to Christ, then you are Abraham's descendants, heirs according to promise.

but the words of the Lord will not pass away.[55] Not one jot or tittle will fail, but the Lord will accomplish all His good pleasure. Therefore, when we look at the glorious end of redemptive history in the book of Revelation, we are reminded that we are beholding the perfect outworking of the Lord's immutable will. What the Lord said He would do has been accomplished through the death of His Son.

- ***The Extent of the Atonement (A Victory of Extensive Redemption):*** Christ came to give His life as a ransom, not for very few, but for many. The extent of Christ's redemptive work is incalculably abundant. Christ's sheep will not only be found in Jerusalem, Judea, and Samaria but also throughout the ends of the earth. The gift that Christ will ultimately give back to the Father will be abundant, beyond human measure (Revelation 7:10). The many for whom Christ died will be there in glory without fail, praising the Lamb for His great and perfect victory for all eternity.

These *victories of Christ* are what centrally define the *intent, immutability,* and *extent* of His atonement. Whatever one might want to believe about the atonement, these truths are utterly unavoidable. But of course, we have not jumped into the boiling pot of the *limited, unlimited* debate. *Absolutely!* You see, it was necessary that we began with these principles of Christ's victory, before entering the lion's den of the contemporary debate. Without these crucial foundations, we may find ourselves being consumed by *human reason and tradition.*

---

[55] Matthew 24:35.

ALL NATIONS UNDER GOD

CHRIST'S VICTORIOUS ATONEMENT

DEFENDED

A Defense, Not a Diatribe

Where no wood is, there the fire goeth out: so where there is no talebearer, the strife ceaseth.
Proverbs 26:20

Did you know that there are people in our country today who are trying to bring back the styles and culture of the 1970's? Yes it is true, and I say to you - WE MUST STOP THEM! I mean, really, wallabies? White leather belts and bell-bottom plaid pants? Even the dreaded lava lamps and avocado-green been bags? The thought of bringing it all back gives me very dark nightmares of light-blue polyester suits and enormous neckties; let's have some mercy here folks! And along with these tortured fashions of that era, there was that popular game that I frankly never liked nor understood: the "Rock'em Sock'em Robots" which consisted of mechanical (plastic) boxing robots that were controlled by two opposing players. The object of the game was, well... to knock your opponent's head clean off (a great game for building relationships). I typically grimaced over this game because whenever my friends actually lured me into a match, it always seemed to degrade to the same experience. It was my goal to play this game as little as possible, because the way to win (I finally learned) was by flailing one's robot with such spastic, unrelenting, mindless force, that the game would end before it had much of a chance to begin. My assessment of it all: this was never a thinking man's game (which is probably why they brought this one back too!). Well, it was all just a game, and no real harm was ever done by it, but in all seriousness I must confess that this childhood memory is, unfortunately, what comes to my mind when I consider some of the atonement debate and rhetoric in the public's view today. I am frankly embarrassed, even ashamed, when I read some of the works that have been published on the subject; too many of these works reduce the dignity of this precious dialogue to a spastic, unrelenting, and robotic rant; and the one who is willing to declare himself the winner in these contests is the one who believes that he has knocked his opponent's head off. But those atonement pundits who wish to engage in a debate over this precious subject ought to keep their conduct and debate in the Spirit and immersed in the profitable Scriptures alone. This warning that I share here is the same one that I have endeavored to apply to myself in this book; thus, in rendering a *defense* of *Christ's victorious atonement*, I have determined to avoid an ungodly *diatribe* of extra-biblical argumentation, undocumented textual criticism, elaborate and emotional illustrations, man-centered logic; and I will not use this as an opportunity to demonize evangelical theologians from church history in some attempt to *knock someone's head off*. These tactics must be avoided for the glory of Christ, for the sake of a genuine search for truth, and for the church's Gospel testimony overall. Mark this: the world watches carefully those who make a profession of Christ. Thus, we can either keep our conduct worthy of the Gospel of Jesus Christ, or blaspheme the fair name and message of the Savior. This is no game. The stakes are very high and our responsibility is quite grave when we seek to defend *the greatest story ever told.* In offering a defense for the doctrine of Christ's victorious atonement, I will present three important arguments from the Scriptures. While there is much more that could be presented for the sake of this discussion, we will keep the matter brief by looking at: 1. *The Lord's justice and mercy;* 2. *His exceptional love for His people; and* 3. *His extensive atonement.* By offering a *defense of doctrine*, our primary focus will be set upon what the Scriptures clearly teach on these subjects; but in addition to these defenses, I have endeavored to anticipate most of the common debates, questions, and oppositions that are most relevant to this important discussion.

A Defense of The Lord's Justice & Mercy

You will say to me then, "Why does He still find fault?
For who resists His will?"
Romans 9:19

Our Scriptural examination of the God-centeredness of the cross was not designed to bypass the important question of mankind's redemption. Not in the least bit! Rather this *theocentricity* of Christ's cross establishes the important truth that our salvation is not the chief end of God. God's chief end, as we have already discussed, is established by Trinitarian love and His eternal glory. Yet, the blessed message of the Bible does not end with this point, but continues with the message of hope for mankind; for the Lord's gracious redemption will extend itself to many throughout all the nations of the earth. This reality of God's gracious redemption is so powerful, so wonderful, and so transcendent, that the human mind is incapable of understanding its fullness. When we consider mankind's nature of sinful corruption, we must understand that God's *decree to save any at all* is a great miracle of love and mercy. What I have said here may shock some readers. If some are shocked, this would be no surprise since many Gospel presentations today are offered in such a way that one would think that mankind is somehow *worthy* of salvation. Yet, this concept has no foundation in the Word of God. In fact, the very meaning of the words *mercy* and *grace* both speak of our *unworthiness* for salvation. Consider the following:

- **Mercy:** H. *hesed* and G. *eleos* denotes the free act of God's restraint, such that He chooses not to give us what we deserve in light of our sin. Thus, the Old Testament's use of *hesed* "mercy" signifies "a kind of love, including ...[*hanûn*], when the object is in a pitiful state."[56] Such kindness is that which is extended to those who are lowly and needy.[57] Thus, Jeremiah reminds us that it is through the Lord's mercies that "we are not consumed."[58] Moving forward to the New Testament, the Apostle Paul instructed Titus concerning God's mercy when he said: "He saved us, not on the basis of deeds which we have done in righteousness, but according to His mercy, by the washing of regeneration and renewing by the Holy Spirit" (Titus 3:5). God's free choice of mercy is therefore the very bedrock of a sinner's temporal preservation[59] or eternal redemption.

- **Grace:** H. *hnăh* and G. *charis* speaks of God's act of freely giving us what we do not deserve, in light of our sin. We are repeatedly taught in the New Testament that salvation is not established by one's personal merit (Ephesians 2:8-9), otherwise grace is no longer grace by definition (Romans 11:6). Thus, the Lord "has saved us and called us with a holy calling, not according to our

---

[56] Harris, R. L., Harris, R. L., Archer, G. L., & Waltke, B. K. (1999, c1980). Theological Wordbook of the Old Testament (electronic ed.) (Page 307). Chicago: Moody Press.

[57] Brown, F., Driver, S. R., & Briggs, C. A. (2000). Enhanced Brown-Driver-Briggs Hebrew and English Lexicon. Strong's, TWOT, and GK references Copyright 2000 by Logos Research Systems, Inc. (electronic ed.) (Page xiii). Oak Harbor, WA: Logos Research Systems.

[58] Lamentations 3:22 Through the Lord's mercies we are not consumed, Because His compassions [*hăsḏey*] fail not. [NKJV]

[59] In Genesis 9:13 the Lord had set His bow in the cloud (the rainbow) as a merciful sign between the Lord and the earth. Though mankind was still desperately wicked, deserving judgment (Genesis 8:21), the Lord established His mercy, signified by the beautiful rainbow. In a sense, the rainbow should remind all the inhabitants of the earth that if it were not for the Lord's undeserved mercy, we would be consumed instantly (Lamentations 3:22). It is a point of bitter irony that the homosexual community has chosen the symbol of the rainbow to represent their corrupt cause; but such a symbol actually gives believers an excellent witnessing opportunity with those who have been given over to such a horrid practice (Romans 1:25-26).

works, but according to His own purpose and grace which was given to us in Christ Jesus before time began" [1 Timothy 1:9, NKJV].

The language of Scripture clearly informs us that mankind does not *deserve* salvation for a very important reason: *indwelling sin*. The Scriptures repeatedly teach us that all have sinned and fall short of God's glory (Romans 3:23); there is none who does good, not even one (Romans 3:12); every intent of the thoughts of man's heart is only evil continually (Genesis 6:5, 8:21); men are dead in their trespasses and sins (Ephesians 2:1-2) and are the children of wrath (Ephesians 2:3); they are even the enemies of God (Romans 5:10) upon whom the judgment and wrath of God abides (John 3:18, 36). Mankind's sinful depravity reminds us that none are *worthy* of salvation, instead, what mankind actually deserves is Hell. This is an important point to be sure. If mankind were somehow innately worthy of salvation, then the very concepts of mercy and grace would be meaningless. In such a system of thought, salvation would simply be the payment for what mankind already deserved in the first place;[60] but this is simply not the case. Therefore, in light of mankind's sin, we understand that had the Lord chosen to save just one member of the human race – that would be great mercy and grace. That it pleased Him to redeem more than one, is even a greater miracle of mercy and grace. *That He has chosen to redeem a great bounty of souls from every tribe, tongue, people and nation – is unspeakable, abounding grace, abundantly beyond all that we could ask or think*! In light of what we deserve, we ought to cry out with loud voices and declare: *grace that is greater than all my sin!* But had we only received the *justice of God*, then all mankind would be

---

[60] Titus 3:5 He saved us, not on the basis of deeds which we have done in righteousness, but according to His mercy, by the washing of regeneration and renewing by the Holy Spirit,

damned forever! But thanks be to God for His unmerited *mercy, grace, and salvation* which abounds in the person of Jesus Christ! In view of all this, would anyone actually dare to argue that God's mercy and grace is somehow without justice? The unfortunate answer to this question is – *yes*. When the apostle Paul wrote to the church at Rome, teaching them about God's immutable promise of redemption, he anticipated the predictable responses of such naysayers:

> *Romans 9:8-16: 8 ...it is not the children of the flesh who are children of God, but the children of the promise are regarded as descendants. 9 For this is a word of promise: "At this time I will come, and Sarah shall have a son." 10 And not only this, but there was Rebekah also, when she had conceived twins by one man, our father Isaac; 11 for though the twins were not yet born, and had not done anything good or bad, in order that God's purpose according to His choice might stand, not because of works, but because of Him who calls, 12 it was said to her, "The older will serve the younger." 13 Just as it is written, "Jacob I loved, but Esau I hated." 14 What shall we say then? There is no injustice with God, is there? May it never be! 15 For He says to Moses, "I will have mercy on whom I have mercy, and I will have compassion on whom I have compassion." 16 So then it does not depend on the man who wills or the man who runs, but on God who has mercy.*

What shall we say in light of this compelling section of Scripture? The one thing that we can't say is that God is unjust, being guilty of any *sin or lie*! Neither can we complain that God has made us into robots, thus resolving an unbiblical form of fatalism - *just as Paul anticipated*:

> *Romans 9:17-20: 17 For the Scripture says to Pharaoh, "For this very purpose I raised you up, to demonstrate My power in you, and that My name might be proclaimed throughout the whole earth." 18 So then He has mercy on whom He desires, and He hardens whom He desires.*

> 19 You will say to me then, "Why does He still find fault? For who resists His will?" 20 On the contrary, who are you, O man, who answers back to God? The thing molded will not say to the molder, "Why did you make me like this," will it?

Paul knew that what he was teaching would provoke two responses from those who might consult their own human reasoning on these matters. It is very likely that the very questions which he anticipated were raised in his day. In like manner, many today reason along the same lines of thinking and ask: "*Is there injustice in God?*" and "*why does He still find fault, for who resists His will?*" In reflecting on the above questions, I am reminded of a saying that is often employed in classroom settings where the teacher will say: "There's no such thing as a bad question." On the contrary, *there is such a thing as a bad question.* Paul refers to these anticipated questions as "*talking back*" to the Potter. It is the complaint of injustice that rebelliously declares "why did you make me like this?" This is the dead end of man-centered pride and human reasoning, and Paul wastes precious little time in rebuking it. What is required when observing the profound truths of God's sovereignty is humility. Paul reminds us in Romans 11:33 that the profound, transcendent truths concerning God's sovereignty and man's responsibility are part of the reason why we all must confess that God's knowledge, His wisdom, His judgments, and His ways are all unsearchable and unfathomable![61] For some, Romans 11:33 is a reason to avoid Paul's important teaching in chapter 9, but this is yet another unfortunate error. While the transcendent truths concerning man's responsibility and God's absolute sovereignty are difficult for the human mind to grasp, they are not any less true. The same can be said of a whole litany of *transcendent doctrines,*

---

[61] Romans 11:33 Oh, the depth of the riches both of the wisdom and knowledge of God! How unsearchable are His judgments and unfathomable His ways!

such as the hypostatic union of Christ, the holy inspiration of Scripture, and even the doctrine of the Trinity. The presence of mystery in any doctrine nullifies nothing, nor does it give us an excuse to avoid these important teachings; instead, the presence of *doctrinal mystery* ought to humble us as we embrace what God has revealed.[62] Having said this, we must not avoid Romans 9, rather we must approach it with submissive hearts. Paul's instructions in this chapter are important because he is establishing the relationship between the promises of God and their effectual outcome. What Paul clearly teaches us is that the immutable outworking of God's predetermined purposes accomplishes a very important thing: *the demonstration of His justice and mercy.* What is often missed, avoided, or bypassed in this remarkable chapter is Paul's use of the inferential particle: *ara*. This particle is frequently used in order to bring a lengthy theological argument to a final conclusion.[63] Conceptually, this is very important and helpful because it is a grammatical tool which helps to bring convergence and finality to any lengthy argument, like Romans 9. You can think of it as a kind of spotlight, designed to highlight a central point of thought. Therefore, here are the Apostle's two highlighted statements in Romans 9:

---

[62] Romans 11:34-35: 34 For who has known the mind of the Lord, or who became His counselor? 35 Or who has first given to Him that it might be paid back to him again?

[63] Romans 8:1 There is *therefore* now no condemnation for those who are in Christ Jesus. Romans 8:1 is the *inferential* conclusion to Paul's prior discourse (at least chapter 7). "*ara*: a marker of result as an inference from what has preceded (frequently used in questions and in the result clause of conditional sentences)— 'so, then, consequently, as a result.'" Louw, J. P., & Nida, E. A. (1996, c1989). Greek-English lexicon of the New Testament : Based on semantic domains (electronic ed. of the 2nd edition.) (Vol. 1, Page 782). New York: United Bible societies.

- *Romans 9:16 So then it does not depend on the man who wills or the man who runs, but on God who has mercy.*

- *Romans 9:18 So then He has mercy on whom He desires, and He hardens whom He desires.*

The words "so then" are the grammatical spotlights for his two, crucial conclusions. What Paul wants his readers to understand is this: God's purposes (according to His choice) will stand, not because of human works, but because of the Lord who calls His people to Himself. God's purposes and promises stand, not by what men do, but by the very power of His decree, therefore *it does not depend on the man who wills or the man who runs, but on God who has mercy.* As if this weren't clear enough, he then concluded that the Lord has mercy on whom He desires and He hardens whom He desires. This statement in verse 18 further affirms what he said in verse 16: Man's redemption depends upon the Lord's mercy – *alone.* Paul then brings closure to this prodigious section of Scripture by affirming God's overall plan of redemption:

Romans 9:22-24: *22 What if God, although willing to demonstrate His wrath and to make His power known, endured with much patience vessels of wrath prepared for destruction? 23 And He did so in order that He might make known the riches of His glory upon vessels of mercy, which He prepared beforehand for glory, 24 even us, whom He also called, not from among Jews only, but also from among Gentiles.*

According to these verses, the Lord's foreordained will was established *in order to display the riches of His glory upon vessels of mercy, which He prepared beforehand for glory.* In all of this, Paul affirms the *theocentricity* of God's redeeming work. As well, he reminds us that the relationship between the promises of God and their ultimate fulfillment is one of *immutability.* Paul also affirms man's dependency upon God's mercy for salvation. If we were tempted to believe that any member of the human race *deserved* mercy, then we might be tempted to join the naysayers and declare that there is injustice in God – but may it never be! The Lord would have been just to have given the whole human race over to its own corruption and judgment,[64] but instead He chose to redeem some upon whom He had sovereignly set His desire. Why He chose *any* for mercy is a great mystery. Why He chose *many* to be redeemed by the blood of the Lamb reveals the great bounty of His kindness. These vessels of mercy are the same ones whom Christ referred to when He said:

> *John 6:38-39: 38 For I have come down from heaven, not to do My own will, but the will of Him who sent Me. 39 And this is the will of Him who sent Me, that of all that He has given Me I lose nothing, but raise it up on the last day.*

Those whom the Father gave to the Son will be raised up on the last day: *not one will be lost*! This disclosure of the Lord's merciful redemption is even more fully developed in the Epistle to the Ephesians. In this Trinitarian doxology, we see the details of the Lord's redemptive work:

- ***The Father's Merciful Choice of Many (1:3-6)*** *He chose us in Him, before the foundation of the world ... to the praise of the glory of His grace, which He freely bestowed on us in the Beloved.*

- ***The Son's Immutable Sacrifice for the Many (1:7-12)*** *In Him, we have redemption through His blood ...that we... would be to the praise of His glory.*

---

[64] Romans 1:18-26.

- ***The Spirit's Sealing and Securing of the Many (1:13-14)*** *In Him... you were sealed with the Holy Spirit ...to the praise of His glory.*

This Trinitarian doxology of Paul's has a very clear agenda; it discloses the glory and grace of the merciful, Triune God. In this text, the Apostle shows us the power of God's will in predestining us to adoption; he then shows us the power of Christ whereby the elect were purchased by His shed blood; and finally he shows us the power of the Holy Spirit as He immutably seals those who are chosen for the day of redemption. Additionally, Paul helps us to understand how the saint's salvation was initiated in the first place. To do this he spotlights the very *willful choice* that began this chain of redemption in the first place:

Ephesians 1:5 He predestined us to adoption as sons through Jesus Christ to Himself, according to the kind intention of His will...

Clearly, it was the kind intention of *His will* that established every aspect of our redemption; or, as we examined before - it is not the man who wills or the man who runs, but God who, according to the kind intention of *His will*, chooses to adopt many for His own glory. These vessels of mercy, whom the Father gave to the Son, will be redeemed without a single flaw or loss.[65] What Paul reveals to us in this text is the exceptional love that was manifested between the Father and the *Beloved One*, Jesus Christ. Those chosen from before the foundation of the world were given to Christ, and Christ, through His sacrifice and resurrection, will yield them back to the Father who gave them in the beginning – that God may be all in all.[66] Here is the great display of God's mercy and justice through

---

[65] John 6:39 This is the will of the Father who sent Me, that of all He has given Me I should lose nothing, but should raise it up at the last day.

[66] 1 Corinthians 15:28.

His kindness and severity: to those who remain in the corruption of their own rebellion – they will face the severity of His just judgment, but to those who are His children, they will taste of His kindness, mercy and grace forever![67]

A Defense of the Lord's Exceptional Love
Jacob I loved, but Esau I hated
Romans 9:13

One of the most important passages in the book of Romans is found towards the end of chapter 11. It is here that the Apostle offers some very powerful reflections, following many transcendent truths concerning the majesty and wonder of God's absolute sovereignty, justice, and mercy:

> *Romans 11:33-36: 33 Oh, the depth of the riches both of the wisdom and knowledge of God! How unsearchable are His judgments and unfathomable His ways! 34 For who has known the mind of the Lord, or who became His counselor? 35 Or who has first given to Him that it might be paid back to him again? 36 For from Him and through Him and to Him are all things. To Him be the glory forever. Amen.*

These verses are the very capstone to the theological building of Romans chapters 1-11. Within these final thoughts of Paul's are some very important expressions of humility, submission, and joy. Despite the naysayers and critics who would accuse him of rendering the Godhead as *unjust* (Romans 9:14) or as being the *author of confusion* (Romans 9:19), Paul ended these deeply challenging chapters with an expression of joyful and humble praise. Paul recognized that when one brings up the important discussion of God's *kindness and severity* (Romans 11:22) that there

---
[67] Romans 11:22.

is something very transcendent about it all; it is a subject of which the human mind has difficulty grasping completely. The words in verse 33 are crucial: *unsearchable* and *unfathomable*. Together they remind any who would be humble enough to admit it that the faculties of the human mind are grossly limited. We can understand many things in Scripture about the nature of God, however, we cannot *search out* or *fathom* the attributes of God in all their fullness. I truly believe that a failure to embrace this crucial expression of humility and submission to God's revelation is the very reason why the descendents of Adam are often prone to accuse God of *injustice* and *confusion*. The human tendency is to balk over the truths of man's responsibility and God's sovereignty. But, instead of refuting God's sovereignty over His creation, the child of God must bow down and confess his frailty, ignorance, and imperfection when beholding these infinite truths. Without such humility and submission, we will surely degrade to a system of thought which expects God's nature and works to fit within the limitations of human logic and thinking. This is, indeed, the natural tendency of all men:

> *Psalm 50:16, 21: 16 ...to the wicked God says... 21 You thought that I was just like you; I will reprove you, and state the case in order before your eyes.*

Left to ourselves, we all tend to degrade the infinite God of the Universe to a *mere man*, in our corrupted and limited thinking. Though such idolatry is normative among men, it is not any less condemnable. A *god* who can entirely fit within the limited cranial space of the human mind is no god at all. Thus, no one is greater than God, and therefore no one can serve as His counselor.[68] His

---

[68] Romans 11:34 For who has known the mind of the Lord, or who became His counselor?

ways are not our ways, nor are His thoughts our thoughts.[69] When armed with such humility and submission to God's Word, we can more easily embrace such challenging texts as Romans 9:13, understanding that the Lord's love is wonderfully multifaceted to such an extent that He even has a *compassionate love* for the rebellious sinners of this world:

> *Matthew 5:43-45: 43 You have heard that it was said, "You shall love your neighbor, and hate your enemy." 44 But I say to you, love your enemies, and pray for those who persecute you 45 in order that you may be sons of your Father who is in heaven; for He causes His sun to rise on the evil and the good, and sends rain on the righteous and the unrighteous.*

Here is a profound text indeed! The children of God are to *love their enemies* so that they may imitate the Father's *universal love*, for He *causes His sun to rise on the evil and the good, and sends rain on the righteous and the unrighteous*. The idea of loving one's enemy is not the product of human logic, but it is an *imitation of God's universal love, which includes a love for those who are His enemies*. God has a love for men who are *evil* and *unrighteous* – even men like Esau! In light of Matthew 5:43-45 it is amazing to consider that the Lord simultaneously hated Esau while bestowing upon him a great bounty of *compassion and love*; this He did upon the very one who desired his forsaken birthright, rather than the Lord Himself.[70] God's love for the godless[71] may be one of the most counter-intuitive facts of Scripture, but this only shows us that *human intuition* is not a trustworthy resource for truth – ever. We must avoid the common error that concludes that God has no love

---

[69] Isaiah 55:8 "For My thoughts are not your thoughts, Neither are your ways My ways," declares the Lord.
[70] Hebrews 12:15-17.
[71] Hebrews 12:16.

for those who are not His own. The Lord's love is patient, kind, and full of compassion. Thus, it is by His *loving patience* that He has endured the many generations of sinful men (1 Peter 3:20);[72] it was by His *lovingkindness* that He appeared to mankind, endowed with salvation[73] (Titus 3:4) and offered the gracious Gospel to all men (Matthew 28:18-20); and it is by His *loving compassion* that He does not delight in the death of the wicked, therefore He graciously calls the wicked to repentance (Ezekiel 18:23). By His perpetual beneficence, all men have physical life[74] and on a daily basis they behold the chorus of praise declared from all creation (Psalm 19:1-6). He showers mankind with the sun and the rain, within this habitable earth which He created for His good pleasure, and which someday will be destroyed with intense heat.[75] Until that day, all men will continue to be the recipients of God's universal love, without exception. And so it is: This love of God is supplied to all men *universally;*[76] however, His *exceptional love* is given *uniquely to those who are in His Son,* so that they would share in His holiness.[77] The Lord's love for His own children is - *exceptional*. It is of the very same quality of unique love that the Father has for his Beloved Son, therefore, the Lord deals with His redeemed *as sons*.

John 15:9 Just as the Father has loved Me, I have also loved you; abide in My love.

---

[72] 1 Peter 3:20 ...when the patience of God kept waiting in the days of Noah, during the construction of the ark, in which a few, that is, eight persons, were brought safely through the water.

[73] Titus 3:4 But when the kindness and the love of God our Savior toward man appeared...

[74] Acts 17:24-25.

[75] 2 Peter 3:9-10.

[76] Matthew 5:44-45.

[77] Hebrews 12:10 For they indeed for a few days chastened us as seemed best to them, but He for our profit, that we may be partakers of His holiness. [NKJV]

Such love from the Father is also a love that supplies the chastening, reproof, and correction that is needed in order to conform His children to the image of Christ Himself. It is called *exceptional* because it is *uniquely given* to those who are His and is withheld from those who are not:

> Hebrews 12:6-8: *6 For whom the Lord loves He chastens, and scourges every son whom He receives. 7 If you endure chastening, God deals with you as with sons; for what son is there whom a father does not chasten? 8 But if you are without chastening, of which all have become partakers, then you are illegitimate and not sons.*

In this important text, we have a clear distinction being made between those who are the sons of God and those who are not. The author of Hebrews wrote the Jewish believers of his day in order to encourage them amidst their suffering and trials; this he did by teaching them about the Lord's *exceptional love* for His own. He explained to them that they had *forgotten the exhortation that was addressed to them as sons;* this exhortation from Proverbs 3:12 teaches us that those *whom the Lord loves, He disciplines.* Conversely, those who are without such loving discipline *are not sons*. Even Christ, the Author of our salvation, was perfected through sufferings[78] such that He *learned obedience through the things which He suffered.*[79] Thus, the Father's *exceptional love* for His own Son stands as the greatest example of the very love that He has for His children:[80] *the Lord loves those whom He reproves*. This distinction of love had a very important message for the 1st century church. For the children of God it was a message of great hope in

---

[78] Hebrews 2:10.
[79] Hebrews 5:8 though He was a Son, yet He learned obedience by the things which He suffered. [NKJV]
[80] Hebrews 2:11 For both He who sanctifies and those who are being sanctified are all of one, for which reason He is not ashamed to call them brethren, [NKJV]

light of the Lord's sovereign purposes in trials and suffering.[81] It was also a message of warning to those who either resisted or did not receive the Lord's loving chastening. Those who were without the Lord's loving chastening, proved themselves to be the contented inhabitants of this fallen world, and thus they were deemed *illegitimate*.[82] These messages of encouragement, and warning, have been necessary for every generation of the church, because it is needful to understand that God's judgment is upon those who are not sons;[83] but to His own sons, the Lord gives His exceptional love. The fact that God's love is distinguishable between those who are sons, and those who are not, constitutes a very important doctrine. But "what son is there whom a father does not chasten?" the author of Hebrews asks. Of course, in our day of undisciplined parents and children, the contemporary answer could be very disappointing; but the biblical answer is – *none*. To leave a child without loving discipline is a hateful thing, and this is not what the Lord does with His own.[84] It is important to remember that this *exceptional love* was established *from before the foundation of the world* when He adopted us as sons by His predetermination and good will.[85] Before His chosen children had done anything good or bad,[86] *in order that God's purpose according to His choice might stand*,[87] the Lord secured them in His exceptional love.[88] We

---

[81] Philippians 1:29 For to you it has been granted on behalf of Christ, not only to believe in Him, but also to suffer for His sake.
[82] G. *nothos* – A bastard; a child born out of wedlock.
[83] John 3:18.
[84] Proverbs 13:24 He who spares his rod hates his son, But he who loves him disciplines him promptly.
[85] Ephesians 1:5 having predestined us to adoption as sons by Jesus Christ to Himself, according to the good pleasure of His will,
[86] Jeremiah 1:4-5: 4 Then the word of the Lord came to me, saying: 5 "Before I formed you in the womb I knew you; 1 Before you were born I sanctified you; I ordained you a prophet to the nations."
[87] Romans 9:11.

see, in the Scriptures, several expressions of this exceptional love, relating to Christ's servanthood and sacrifice which was made on behalf of those whom the Father gave to Him:

- *Christ, A Servant for His Friends:* Christ taught His disciples that there is no greater love than when one *lays down his life for his friends (John 15:13).* "You did not choose Me, but I chose you and appointed you that you should go and bear fruit," the Savior declared to them; and then He commanded them, a few verses later, to "love one another" (John 15:16-17). And who were the Lord's friends? He clarified this, wonderfully, when He declared: "you are my friends if you do what I command you" (John 15:14). Here we see that Christ's *exceptional love* was uniquely set upon a particular people: genuine believers (John 14:21). Judas, the son of perdition,[89] was clearly not one of those who *did what Christ commanded.* Thus, Christ's exceptional love is only for those who would hear Him, believe in Him, and do what He commanded.

- *Christ, the Good Shepherd of His Sheep:* Christ's exceptional love for His own is also defined in terms of this relationship of a shepherd and his sheep: "I am the good shepherd; and I know My sheep, and am known by My own" (John 10:14). As we learned from John chapter 15, Christ's sacrifice on His disciples' behalf was an act of exceptional love. However, there are those who were not the recipients of His atoning work; these are individuals who are not His sheep: "But you do not believe, because you are not of My sheep, as I said to you" [John 10:26, NKJV]. Consider this important passage for a moment. He did not say that they were not His sheep *because* they did not believe. Rather He said that they did not believe *because they were not His sheep.* The

---

[88] Romans 9:13 As it is written, "Jacob I have loved, but Esau I have hated."
[89] John 17:12 "While I was with them in the world, I kept them in Your name. Those whom You gave Me I have kept; and none of them is lost except the son of perdition, that the Scripture might be fulfilled."

order here is important. Those who rejected Him did so because they were not Christ's to begin with. But Christ's own sheep are the undeserved recipients of divine mercy and grace, therefore they *hear His voice and follow Him.* Here again are the wonderful pictures of the Lord's effectual calling, and His exceptionally loving sacrifice that was made on behalf of His own.

- ***Christ, the Bridegroom of His Bride:*** The Apostle Paul presents an important portrait of exceptional, monogamous love, in his epistle to the church at Ephesus. The very bride that was given to the Son before the foundation of the world (Ephesians 1:4-5) *was the only one who was in view when He gave up His life as a sacrifice for sin.* This portrait of unique love gives Paul's instruction to husbands a great deal of depth and meaning. Husbands are to imitate Christ in His unique and exceptional love for the church, for His was a pure and *monogamous love*: "Husbands, love your wives, just as Christ also loved the church and gave Himself for her..." (Ephesians 5:25). Such a precious vision of Christ's *exceptional love* gives husbands an important standard for their fidelity to their own wives.

- ***Christ, the Priest of His people:*** As a Son, and a priest, Christ learned obedience through suffering, and became "the source of eternal salvation to all who obey Him;" this, Christ did "...according to the order of Melchizedek" (Hebrews 5:8-9, NKJV). By His "one offering He has perfected forever those who are being sanctified" (Hebrews 10:14). His unique love was expressed as a priest for those who were under His ministerial watchcare, therefore, "Christ was offered once to bear the sins of many. To those who eagerly wait for Him He will appear a second time, apart from sin, for salvation..." (Hebrews 9:28, NKJV).[90] His priestly sacrifice was offered once, for all time, on behalf of His

---

[90] Hebrews 7:25 Hence, also, He is able to save forever those who draw near to God through Him, since He always lives to make intercession for them.

friends, who are also known as His *sheep* and *bride*. Here is exceptional love for those who are His own!

The vessels of mercy whom the Father adopted and gave to the Son, from before the foundation of the world, *will be immutably* redeemed, protected, and resurrected into glory, *to the praise of the glory of His grace, which He freely bestowed on us in the Beloved*. It was by the exercise of His merciful will that not all would be lost, but that many would be redeemed by the blood of the Lamb; and this choice of the Father's was done *before any were born, and had not done anything good or bad, in order that God's purpose according to His choice might stand*. Indeed, there is no injustice in God; rather He abounds with great mercy and love!

A Defense of the Lord's Extensive Atonement

And other sheep I have which are not of this fold; them also I must bring, and they will hear My voice; and there will be one flock and one shepherd.
John 10:16 [NKJV]

Can it be said that Christ's atonement was universal? Well, when we consider the song of the Lamb in Revelation 5:6-10, it is obvious that His atonement was *incomprehensibly extensive*, but it clearly was not universal. Because of this, there is a great problem that comes with arguing that the atonement was originally universal, *in its intent*, but not universal *in its effect*. If this were the case, one would have to wonder why Christ would be called the Victor. The Savior promised that He would lose nothing but raise it up on the last day;[91] thus, how can Christ's atoning work on the cross be counted as *infallible* within the reasoning of *universalism?* This question is worthy of our time and attention in light of the regular assertions made by the advocates of universal atonement. It is not

---
[91] John 6:38-39.

my assertion that all the advocates of universalism are intentionally trying to deny the infallibility of Christ and His work; the Lord knows their hearts as I cannot. However, there is a great need to scrutinize such teaching in light of the text of Scripture, in order to see if the atonement is ever presented as having a universal design, or not. The implications of our conclusion would in no way be small, but vastly significant since they ultimately impact our understanding of God's oaths and promises - even the very nature of God Himself. In the overall atonement debate, there are several key texts which are typically contested. This is most often the case because of language that is used in order to describe the extensive nature of Christ's sacrificial work. In many cases, such verses are mistakenly advanced as supporting material for an unlimited atonement. At the center of all this confusion is a common collection of words which are often used to speak of the vast nature of God's grace as it is extended throughout the world. These words are (typically): *all, many, every, world, men and mankind*. To begin our examination of these words, we'll begin with a very common example of two relevant passages:

> *Mark 10:45: 45 For even the Son of Man did not come to be served, but to serve, and to give His life a ransom for many. [NKJV]*

> *1 Timothy 2:6: 5 For there is one God and one Mediator between God and men, the Man Christ Jesus, 6 who gave Himself a ransom for all, to be testified in due time... [NKJV]*

Texts like these are often found in the midst of the atonement tug of war; after all, did He die for *many* or for *all?* Typical lexical analyses of the Greek word *all*, in all its varied forms [*pas, pasa, pan, pantas*], whether it has an article or not (arthrous or anarthrous),[92] show that the word takes on several different meanings, depending upon its contextual use.[93] There are *at least* 6 different possible uses of the anarthrous "all" and *at least* 3 different uses in the arthrous setting.[94] As it is true for any serious study of Scripture, context must establish the proper understanding of any word and its use. However, a common misunderstanding is that the word "all" should be understood with a universal connotation, without exception. While there are many important uses of a universal "all" in Scripture, this is not the exclusive meaning of the word. Let us consider the variability of this word by first looking at the word "all" as it denotes the concept of absolute universality – that is, *all without exception*:

Scriptural use of "All"	Meaning/Concept: *All Without Exception*
John 10:29: My Father, who has given them to Me, is greater than all; and no one is able to snatch them out of the Father's hand.	The Lord's greatness over *all things* is incontestable. In view of the Lord's Omnipotence it is necessary to understand the word *all* as an absolutely universal expression for He is greater than all *without exception*.
Acts 1:24 And they prayed, and said, "Thou, Lord, who knowest the hearts of all men..."	By the analogy of Scripture it is clearly understood that the Lord, in His Omniscience, knows the hearts and minds of all men *without exception*.
Ephesians 1:21: [Christ has been exalted] far above all rule and authority and power and dominion, and every name that is named, not only in this age but also in the one to come.	Christ's eternal exaltation, far above all rule and authority and power and dominion, and every name that is named, stands as a glorious and unqualified reality. There is no authority or dominion or power that exists apart from Christ. Here again, only a universal all will make sense in this important text.

---

[92] A substantive that is preceded by an article is said to be *arthrous*, whereas one that lacks the article is *anarthrous*.
[93] Friberg, T., Friberg, B., & Miller, N. F. (2000). Vol. 4: Analytical lexicon of the Greek New Testament. Baker's Greek New Testament library. Grand Rapids, Mich.: Baker Books.
[94] Ibid.

When the word *all* is used with respect to God's attributes, then the concept of universality is *usually* in force; and yet this is not always the case either. For example, the Lord is called Almighty [*pantōkratōr*[95] – Literally: *all*-might] and yet we know that His might and power are never used *in order to lie or commit sin*; hence, He has all power, but only that which is *consistent with His holy nature*. To treat every use of *all* as being absolutely universal (i.e., having no exceptions) can be quite hazardous, and it defies the manner in which the word has been used throughout history. As we mentioned before, context is crucial in understanding the multifaceted use of the word *all*, therefore, the reader must pay careful attention to how the author is employing the word in its setting. To illustrate this point, let us consider an important example that is given to us by Christ in John 12:32, just after the Pharisees observed that "the world" had gone after Him in verse 19 of the same chapter:

> John 12:32: *"And I, if I am lifted up from the earth, will draw all peoples to Myself."*

If one were to force the word *all* to mean *all men universally (without exception)*, then some very significant problems crop up immediately. On the one hand, a universal *all* begs the question of *Universalism*; that is, the doctrine which teaches that *all mankind* is, or will be, saved. But such teaching is clearly unbiblical and not worthy of refutation.[96] Moreover, an assumption of Universalism raises other questions: if *all* are thought to be drawn by a mere *external call*, then what can be said about the vast numbers who

---

[95] The very name "Almighty" is a contraction of two Greek words: *pantas* [all] + *kratos* [might/power]. God does have all might and power, but it is important to remember that this power is always in perfect agreement with His holy and righteous nature.

[96] Revelation 20:11-15.

have never heard the Gospel message? After all, no man can be drawn to Christ apart from the Scriptures, *for the Gospel is essential for God's work of drawing men to Christ - without it, there can be no salvation*:

> Romans 10:14: *How then shall they call on Him in whom they have not believed? And how shall they believe in Him of whom they have not heard? And how shall they hear without a preacher?*

Romans 10:14 teaches us that for men to be drawn to Christ, the Scriptures must be presented[97] so that the sinner might be led to the true object of faith: the Lord Jesus Christ.[98] Therefore, this important observation raises a question regarding the use of a universal *all* in John 12:32: if Christ, after His crucifixion, would draw *all men without exception,* then how is it that the Gospel message has never spanned the globe? Certainly, the Gospel had extended throughout the Roman Empire within the first few hundred years, but it certainly was not universal by that time. It then progressed throughout Europe and the Far East in the successive generations; but while the message of the Gospel has been spreading for over 2000 years, it is still not the case that men from every tribe, tongue, people, and nation have heard the Gospel. In fact, there have been scores of people, throughout the globe, who have perished without the Gospel ever reaching their ears. The spread of the Gospel has been remarkable indeed, but it has never been absolutely universal - even to this day. Therefore, by forcing the word *all* to mean *all without exception*, strange conclusions are produced.[99] However, if we take *all* to mean *all without distinction*,

---

[97] The Father draws men to His Son through the Scriptures which testify of Him (John 6:45).

[98] James 1:18 Of His own will He brought us forth by the word of truth, that we might be a kind of firstfruits of His creatures.

[99] John 6:44, 65.

then suddenly the text has relevant meaning, both by itself, and within its own context. I say *within its context* because prior to Christ's profound declaration in verse 32, the Pharisees had been complaining about the *extensive nature of His ministry:*

> John 12:19 *The Pharisees therefore said among themselves, "You see that you are accomplishing nothing. Look, the world has gone after Him!"*

The *world* had gone after Him! Here is yet another example of a word that expresses the idea of *extensiveness*, not absolute universality. Who in their right mind would assume that *all humanity* (without exception) followed Christ in Jerusalem that day? This would be a ridiculous conclusion. What was meant in their statement is as follows: *all walks of life* were following Christ; some were Jews[100] and others were Gentiles.[101] His ministry not only impacted the Jewish and Samaritan communities,[102] but also many Greeks, which broadly categorizes *all other nations and ethnicities.* Therefore, a*ll kinds of humanity* were following Christ. It was therefore in this very context that Christ declared that He *would draw all* throughout the earth. In keeping with the effectual drawing mentioned in John 6:44 & 65, this promise looks to the *actual salvation of all kinds and classes of humanity.* This is exactly what the Good Shepherd said He would do by His immutable promise, just a few chapters earlier in John's Gospel:

---

[100] John 12:11 because on account of him many of the Jews went away and believed in Jesus.

[101] John 12:20-21 20 Now there were certain Greeks among those who came up to worship at the feast.21 Then they came to Philip, who was from Bethsaida of Galilee, and asked him, saying, "Sir, we wish to see Jesus."

[102] John 4.

John 10:16 And I have other sheep, which are not of this fold; I must bring them also, and they shall hear My voice; and they shall become one flock with one shepherd.

Christ's sheep have been chosen of the Father such that *the many* will include not only the remnant of Israel, but also many Gentiles throughout the whole world. And the Lord's work of drawing His sheep is proven to be immutably effectual, because they will hear His voice and will become one flock with one Shepherd! These contextual considerations are crucial and they help us greatly with our understanding of John 12:32. In light of Christ's immutable victory, we see biblical consistency between the *intent* and the *effect* of the Lord's will. Christ's promised work of the cross is the *condition*, and His work of effectual drawing is the stated *conclusion*:

John 12:32

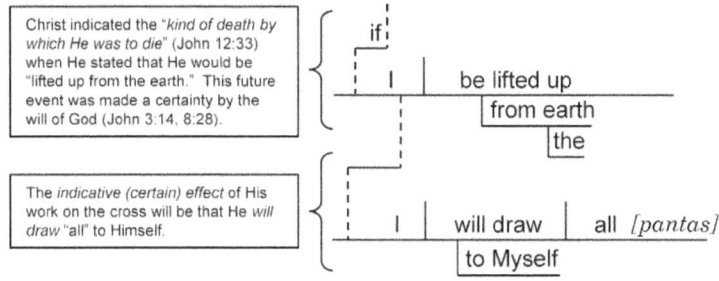

The truths concerning Christ's certain death, as well as His effectual drawing of His sheep to Himself, are wonderfully supplied in this single verse. The broad reference of *all [pantas]* depicts the expansive nature of Christ's future and effectual drawing. The significance of this language in John 12:32 is explained further by John Owen in his classic work – *The Death of Death in the Death of Christ*:

"Then who, I pray, are these all? Are they all and every one? Then are all and every one drawn to Christ, made believers, and truly converted, and shall be certainly saved; for those that come unto Him by His and His Father's drawing, 'He will in no wise cast out," John vi. 37. All, then, can here be no other than many, some of all sorts, no sort excluded..."[103]

The absolute relationship between Christ's certain work on the cross, and His effectual work of drawing all who are His, is crucial for understanding the certainty of His oaths and promises, for what the Lord intends to do He effectually does, by His sovereign power:

> Intent[(His many sheep - John 6-12)] » Effect[(Many - Rev. 5:5-10)] = **Victorious Atonement**

Conversely, any attempt to impose the meaning of all without exception (universalism), upon texts which speak of Christ's redemptive work, raises serious questions and concerns regarding Christ's declared victory in Revelation 5. If the intent of the cross was designed to bring about the *actual redemption* of *all men without exception*, then something has gone wrong. An objective such as this does not find fulfillment in such a scheme. Whatever motives that one might have in upholding this form of universalism, it is quite certain that such a view does not comport with the reality of Christ's infallible work. But when we understand that Christ gave His life as a ransom for *many*, that is, men of *all kinds throughout the earth*, then the relationship between His promise, and the fulfillment of His promise, is powerfully affirmed:

---

[103] Dr. Owen then cites the song of the Lamb as an illustration of Christ's point in John 12:32, with a resolve of praise for Christ's vast and extensive atonement: "Rev. v. 9, 'Thou has redeemed us out of every kindred, and tongue, and people, and nation.' These are the all He draws to Him: which exposition of this phrase is with me of more value and esteem than a thousand glosses of the sons of men." Owen, The Death of Death, p. 308.

Mark 10:45 "For even the Son of Man did not come to be served, but to serve, and to give His life a ransom for many."

> Intent^(Many - Mark 10:45) ≫ Effect^(Many - Rev. 5:5-10) = Victorious Atonement

The language of this verse is compelling. Christ came into the world with a specific mission. This indicative aorist verb in Mark 10:45 establishes the *certainty* of His mission in life: He *came* to serve and to give His life as a ransom for many. This indicative mission of the Son was to procure the redemption of many, that is, a vast supply of men and women throughout all the world. This clear understanding of Christ's mission is entirely consistent with the original declaration of His mission, given when He was born. When we recall that an angel of the Lord announced that *indicative* promise, declaring that the incarnate Christ *will save* (*sōsei*)[104] His people from their sins, we are thus reminded that Christ's promises were fulfilled *victoriously* and *flawlessly*. By comparing the language of Mark 10:45 and Matthew 1:21 with the song of the Lamb, it is quite clear that the heavenly celebration of Revelation 5 centers on the *unerring and extensive victory of Jesus Christ*! From beginning to end, the atonement of Christ is consistently spoken of in terms of its *extensive and bountiful nature*. C. H. Spurgeon has shared some helpful thoughts on this very subject:

"the whole world has gone after him" Did all the world go after Christ? "then went all Judea, and were baptized of him in Jordan." Was all Judea, or all Jerusalem, baptized in Jordan? "Ye are of God, little

---

[104] Matthew 1:21 "And she will bring forth a Son, and you shall call His name Jesus, for He will save His people from their sins." Here again, the indicative verb speaks of real action rather than hypothetical or potential action. Christ's mission was rendered a certainty by the unerring will of God.

children", and the whole world lieth in the wicked one". Does the whole world there mean everybody? The words "world" and "all" are used in some seven or eight senses in Scripture, and it is very rarely the "all" means all persons, taken individually. The words are generally used to signify that Christ has redeemed some of all sorts -- some Jews, some Gentiles, some rich, some poor, and has not restricted His redemption to either Jew or Gentile."[105]

The careful student of Scripture must cautiously examine not only the words of Scripture, but their contexts as well. With this in view, it is important to remember that with any word which speaks of the *extent* of God's redemption, or even the *extent* of man's sinfulness, great care must be given in order to comprehend just *how broad that extent is* - all men in the world are sinful, but not all are redeemed. Because of the multiple references to Christ's vast redemption, and man's universal sin, it is very important for the reader to understand the varied uses of the words: *many, all, the world and even the whole world.* In particular, the word *world* is often misunderstood since it can take on several different meanings:[106] 1. The concept of order (as in a woman's adornment); 2. All created beings within the universe; 3. The world within the general sphere of creation; 4. All men without distinction; 5. The world as inhabited by mankind; 6. The world of sinful humanity; and 7. The world *order* as governed by evil deeds or doctrines (or both).

Consider the following examples:

---

[105] Sermon #181, Matthew 20:28, Delivered on Sabbath Morning, February 28, 1858 by the REV. C. H. Spurgeon at the Music Hall, Royal Surrey Gardens.

[106] Owen, The Death of Death, *Book IV.* pp. 294-403.

Scriptural use of "World"	Meaning/Concept
John 1:10 He was in the world, and the world was made through Him, and the world did not know Him.	The very ones who did not *know Christ*, when *He was in the world*, were unbelievers (John 16:3). Clearly, His true disciples knew Him and believed in Him, therefore this reference to *the world (that did not know Him)* is a reference to the *world of men* who remain at enmity with God (John 3:36).
1 John 5:19 We know that we are of God, and the whole world lies in the power of the evil one.	The believer is no longer under Satan's power or dominion (Colossians 1:13), therefore John's reference to "the whole world" is a general reference to *the sinful world order under Satan's power.*
Colossians 1:5-6: you previously heard ... the gospel, 6 which has come to you, just as in all the world...	Paul said that the Gospel had come to *all the world [panti tō kosmō]*. Paul wrote his letter to the Colossians somewhere between 60-62 A.D. By this time the Gospel message had made great progress, but Paul is clearly not saying that the world *without exception* had been evangelized by then! His point is that the Gospel was making vast, *even extensive progress throughout the world.*
1 John 2:2 and He Himself is the propitiation for our sins; and not for ours only, but also for those of the whole world.	To John's limited audience of churches in Asia Minor, he offered a reminder of the *extensive nature of Christ's powerful atonement.* Christ's propitiatory sacrifice was not only for them *in their day*, but was for all the children of God who were scattered abroad throughout the world and would *someday be drawn to the Good Shepherd as the Gospel mission progressed* (John 11:50-52).

1 John 2:2 is a classic example of the need for careful consideration concerning the extensiveness of the text. In many respects, John's message here is reflective of the message which he presented in John chapter 11. In both cases, we have a great message of hope in light of the shed blood of Christ. In John chapter 11 we see that the Lord sovereignly used the mouth of Caiaphas to utter an important prophecy. This prophecy conveyed the extensive nature of Christ's redeeming work that would extend far beyond the boundaries of Israel:

John 11:50-52 ...it is expedient for you that one man should die for the people, and that the whole nation should not perish. 51 Now this he did not say on his own authority; but being high priest that year he prophesied that Jesus would die for the nation, 52 and not for that nation only, but also that He would gather together in one the children of God who were scattered abroad.

Christ's atoning sacrifice would not only redeem many in Israel (the *whole* nation will not perish), but there were many of God's children *scattered abroad* who would someday hear the Gospel and be redeemed. Therefore, Christ's sacrifice would extensively impact *many throughout the whole world.* John's record of this event is, in many ways, reflected in his exhortation in 1 John 2:2. His readers in Asia Minor needed the reminder that the Gospel ministry of the church would not end until all the sheep of Christ were gathered throughout the whole world. A message such as this was an important message of hope, for in his day the disciples of Christ had endured much in the way of external persecutions and internal heresies. The Gospel had already spread through most of the Roman Empire, but it still was advancing in its infancy. John wanted his readers to remember that the redemptive effect of Christ's shed blood would be seen *extensively throughout the whole world* such that some day many men out of every tribe, tongue, people, and nation would be gathered into the Savior's bosom, as Owen observes:

> *"...by the whole world in this [1 John 2:2] can nothing be understood but men living throughout the whole world, in all the parts and regions thereof (in opposition to the inhabitants of any one nation, place, or country, as such), as the redeemed of Christ are said to be, Rev. v. 9."*[107]

What is often missed in texts such as 1 John 2:2 is the *missiology* that is presented. The church must never lose sight of her perpetual mission to the world *without distinction of race, class, ethnicity or*

---

[107] Owen, The Death of Death, p. 330.

geography. The world will remain a perpetual mission field until the Lord returns for His people. This was the necessary message to the 1st century church and it remains as a crucial doctrine for us as well. God is not a respecter of persons. He does not redeem men from only a few nations and classes, therefore, the church's Gospel *mission* must always be indiscriminate, as unto the whole world:

> *1 Timothy 2:1-6: Therefore I exhort first of all that supplications, prayers, intercessions, and giving of thanks be made for **all** men, 2 for kings and **all** who are in authority, that we may lead a quiet and peaceable life in all godliness and reverence. 3 For this is good and acceptable in the sight of God our Savior, 4 who desires **all** men to be saved and to come to the knowledge of the truth. 5 For there is one God and one Mediator between God and men, the Man Christ Jesus, 6 who gave Himself a ransom for **all**, to be testified in due time [NKJV].*

In this example, we see the Apostle Paul teaching young Timothy concerning the church's breadth of ministry. Paul's first instruction to Timothy was to pray for *all* men. This wasn't a command to lay hold of a worldwide phone book and begin a prayer ministry for every living human being on the earth, *by name*. Instead, his qualification in verse 2 is important: *all men...for kings and all who are in authority*. Clearly, kings and men in authority do not comprise *all men* in a universal sense. What Paul is teaching Timothy is very important: Timothy was not to pray only for the common people of his own community, but he was to extend his entreaties on behalf of *men of all kinds and classes* - this would include the likes of Emperor Nero who was ruling at the time of this epistle. The implicit reminder that Paul therefore supplies is that *God is not a respecter of persons*. The Lord is powerful to save those who even lived as the hostile enemies of the cross – just as Paul did before his conversion (1 Timothy 1:12-14). Hence, the context of Paul's message in 1 Timothy 2:1-3 then flows to his statements in verses 4-6; the Lord's powerful grace not only works in the lives of men and women from the common classes, but He can even bring to repentance horrifically wicked men like Nero! This is the very concept of *all without distinction*, meaning that Christ's redemption applies to people of all *kinds*, without the distinction of their class, age, sex, race or background. This is a very common use of the word *all*, and is found in many more contexts and uses.[108] Paul's important message is the same message of John and of Christ. The shed blood of the Lamb of God has been poured out in vast supply, being generously applied, not to a few, but to many throughout the whole world: to slaves, freedmen, kings, servants, Jews, Barbarians, Scythians, male, female, the rich and the poor from every nation, tribe, tongue and people; all to the praise of His glorious grace! Behold the Lamb of God who takes away the sin of the world!

"Victory" Means "Victory" All of the Time

These shall make war with the Lamb, and the Lamb shall gain the victory over them because He is Lord of lords and King of kings, and they shall also gain the victory who are with Him, the called and the chosen and the faithful.[109]
Revelation 17:14

In the first chapter, I mentioned that I had some discouraging encounters with as a pastor over the subject of the atonement. There, the vehemence that was poured out over the subject of the

---

[108] "...1 Tim. Ii. 4, ... 'God will have all men to be saved,' – in to the sense we give, namely, verse 8, 'I will, therefore, that men pray *en panti topō*' which, that it cannot signify every individual place in heaven, earth, and hell, is of all confessed, and needeth no proof; no more than when our Savior is said to cure *pasan noson*, as Matt. Ix. 35, there is need to prove that he did not cure every disease of every man, but only all sorts of diseases." Owen, The Death of Death, p. 308.

[109] Wuest, K. S. (1997, c1961). The New Testament : An expanded translation. First published in 3 vols., 1956-59, Grand Rapids, MI: Eerdmans.

atonement was deeply troubling. But what I must add is this: there are many more churches that I have encountered that are disturbingly similar. There are many today who have become militant over this debate such that the defense of their conviction is actually more of an angry diatribe. As I have had opportunity to speak with many individuals of this stripe, I find a great commonality among them. Oftentimes, the doctrinal appeals that they make are made based upon just one or two attributes of God. "Why would a *loving* God do 'xyz'?" they often ask. However, speculative questions, which forgo a host of God's other attributes (God's justice, righteousness and wrath), are not spiritually productive. Besides, the study of Scripture must take precedence over entertaining hypothetical speculations. Another refrain that I often hear is this: "All means 'all', all of the time!" As I have already explained, the word *all* has variant forms and meanings, depending on the context in which it is used. Therefore, any attempt to avoid careful and serious study of Scripture is only harmful. In this case, I will carefully invoke the *universal all* and say that such *unscriptural* rhetoric like this is *always harmful.* In reality there are not a great number of words, in either the Hebrew, Greek, or English language, that *always* have the same meaning every time. But there is a biblical word that is wonderfully convergent in its meaning, while being very useful for our discussion of the atonement; it is the word *victory*. Lexically speaking, victory means – *victory.* When you think about it, there aren't many possible variations that such a word could adopt, since it is reduced to the binary thought of victory as opposed to defeat. In light of this we can easily argue that Christ's victory means victory *all of the time.* Antithetically, we must never suggest that there is any failure of mission in Christ's work in the cross. The infallible Song of the Lamb gives us that eternal affirmation that Christ is the victor through His death on the cross. However, it must be stated that a denial of any form of universalism does not signify a denial of the atonement's great abundance. If the Scriptures emphasize anything, they regularly herald the vast bounty that the Messiah's sacrifice brings. Therefore, when the Scriptures speak *specifically of the atonement*, the words used to describe its *extent* are those which depict great abundance.[110] This is especially the case with regard to the songs of worship in the book of Revelation. What a corruption it would be to rephrase the Song of the Lamb to say: "You were slain, and purchased for God a very *limited* number of people throughout history." While it is true, that compared to the vast sea of humanity throughout history, Christ's sheep are much fewer in number, for *many are called but few are chosen* (Matthew 22:14); however the Scriptural assessment of the atonement *mostly fixates on its abundant effect* rather than its *limitation*. Therefore, the Son of Man did not say that He came to give His life as a ransom for a *few*, but for *many*. Paul taught Timothy that Christ's atoning sacrifice can and will save an abundance of men from *all classes of humanity*, even kings and those in authority (1 Timothy 2:1-6). John wrote to the churches of Asia, reminding them that Christ was the propitiation for sin, not only for them in their little corner of the world, but ultimately for a vast number throughout the whole world.[111] Christ's flesh was to be given as bread, not just for the Jewish nation, but for an entire world of believers.[112] The repeated message of the extensive nature of the atonement reminds us that mankind has been given an abundance of grace and mercy and that God is not a respecter of persons. The grace and mercy that He has given will always be more than what we deserve, because what all

---

[110] Mark 10:45; Matthew 20:28; 1 Timothy 2:1-6; 1 John 2:2, 4:14.
[111] 1 John 2:12.
[112] John 3:16, 6:51 "I am the living bread which came down from heaven. If anyone eats of this bread, he will live forever; and the bread that I shall give is My flesh, which I shall give for the life of the world."

the descendents of Adam deserve is eternal condemnation. What Adam did for those who were his (*the fallen human race*) is nothing but sinful failure; but what Christ did for those who were His (*those chosen of the Father*) resulted in righteous victory. This is Paul's clear assessment in Romans 5:15-19:

	Adam's Gift of Corruption *To His Progeny* *(The Human Race)*	*Christ's Gift of Justification* *To His Progeny* *(His Chosen Race)*
15	(a) ...the free gift is not like the offense. For if by the one man's offense **many** died...	(b) ...much more the grace of God and the gift by the grace of the one Man, Jesus Christ, abounded to **many**...
16	(a) And the gift is not like that which came through the one who sinned. For the judgment which came from one offense resulted in condemnation...	(b) ...but the free gift which came from many offenses resulted in justification...

The contrast that Paul supplies by comparing the first Adam to the Last Adam is one of *failure* versus *victory*. Adam's sin effectually supplied nothing but corruption to his progeny: the human race. But Christ's gift effectually supplies grace to the many who are His.

The results of these gifts of corruption (from Adam) and grace (from Christ) are then delineated in the verses that follow:

	Adam's Effectual Failure *For His Progeny* *(The Human Race)*	*Christ's Effectual Victory* *For His Progeny* *(His Chosen Race)*
17	(a) For if by the one man's offense death reigned through the one...	(b) ...much more those who receive abundance of grace and of the gift of righteousness will reign in life through the One, Jesus Christ...
18	(a) Therefore, as through one man's offense judgment came to all men, resulting in condemnation...	(b) ...even so through one Man's righteous act the free gift came to all men, resulting in justification of life...
19	(a) For as by one man's disobedience many were made sinners...	(b) ...so also by one Man's obedience many will be made righteous...

Verses 18 and 19 form an important unit since they present the *inferential conclusion*[113] to his overall comparison of the first and last Adam. Paul indicates that through Christ's one righteous act, the free gift came to all men, resulting in justification of life. It cannot be said that all men *without exception* receive justification of life – this would amount to *absolute Universalism*; thus, this is not his point. Clearly, Paul's reference to *all men* (v. 18b) is clarified as being the *many* who are His and who will be made righteous by His shed blood (v. 19b). Thus, Adam's one act led to condemnation for *all* his progeny (mankind), but Christ's bounty of grace resulted in justification of life for *all* His progeny (His chosen people).[114] By this we are reminded that Christ's stewardship towards the human race stands in direct contrast to Adam's failed stewardship. Christ's stewardship was one of righteous conquest, but Adam's was of sinful defeat. What Christ did on the cross resulted in the redemption of the many for whom He died, such that all who are His *will be justified* by His sacrifice. This is the same victorious message of the song of our Lord Jesus Christ as found in Revelation 5:9-10, and it is a meditation that should fill us with unspeakable joy, excitement, and greater love for Him.

May the church of Jesus Christ humbly submit to the Lord and His revelation, and give thanks to Him for His vast supply of grace and mercy that has been given to the many for whom Christ died.

---

[113] Verse 18 begins with Paul's familiar inferential particle *ara* and is conjoined to verse 19 with the connective particle *ṓsper*.

[114] Matthew 1:21.

All Nations Under God

Christ's Victorious Atonement Applied

Listening to the Victorious Lamb
"This is My Son, My Chosen One;
listen to Him!"
Luke 9:35

The culture of modern Christianity is a busy, bustling synergy, filled with many programs, curricula, Bible studies, seminars, books, and radio preachers. Of course, it is not that seminars, books, radio preachers, and programs are inherently bad; but what has become problematic, in most cases, is that many people have become dependent upon this kind of programmatic-Christianity to such an extent that their "spirituality" actually depends upon it. Such patterns of life resultantly exalt religious activity above simple devotion to the Lord. Of what I have seen of the spiritual landscape here in America, much of this has become commonplace. The American church may be busier than ever before, but I remain incredulous to the thought that it is more spiritual. On the contrary, I am sadly convinced that the church has become more like busy Martha, and less like Mary, through the lack resolve to sit at the feet of the Savior and quietly listen to Him. Perhaps even Martha is too good of an example for our purposes here; instead, the picture of the modern church is actually more like that of Eve who chatted freely with the Devil in the garden, having no real sense of any danger as she did so:

> *2 Corinthians 11:3 But I am afraid, lest as the serpent deceived Eve by his craftiness, your minds should be led astray from the simplicity and purity of devotion to Christ.*

The modern church has become like those at Corinth, who like Eve, flirted with evil by conversing with those who deserved nothing but a rebuke. In many ways, the modern church has been carelessly chatting with the world and allowing the corruptions of deception to enter into her privileged worship. As a result, the church is more like the world: busy, bustling, deceived and utterly distracted. The great challenge that the church has before her is to restore the simplicity and purity of devotion to Christ by returning to the feet of the Savior in order to listen to Him, *alone.*

Returning to my mention of conflict over the subject of the atonement, I must say that, in my personal experiences, such aggravated conversations almost always came into being, not because I brought up the subject myself, but because others felt compelled to engage in a debate with me. I point this out in order to say that such doctrinal debate is not some hobby horse for me. I do not delight in robotic contests which involve the fruitless matter of wrangling over words. Fixations such as these often point to other spiritual problems, therefore Paul warned Timothy concerning this deadly disease in the church:

> *2 Timothy 2:14 Remind them of these things, and solemnly charge them in the presence of God not to wrangle about words, which is useless, and leads to the ruin of the hearers.*

What can be said of the *conduct* of those who engage in such wrangling over words? *It is useless.* Hence, my motivation to write on this subject comes more as a reaction to the contemporary infighting that is taking place in many churches. I am always broken hearted when I hear of churches that are being divided over a very limited discussion of the doctrine of Christ's atonement, while failing to behold the victorious Lamb of God amidst it all. Such attention to useless wrangling often produces a distraction from Christ's true glory and mission. But what is even more disturbing than the content of these debates themselves is the gracelessness and anger that often ensues among many in the church. I cannot begin to catalogue the number of people I have encountered, who have offered a very animated fight on behalf of hypercalvinism or universalism; and yet the argumentative spirits of these individuals seemed to defy the very grace of which they spoke. In my experience in the ministry I have found that many of these same people, whose appetite consisted of wrangling about words, were very troubled people in their personal lives via marital problems, depression, inconsistent personal priorities, and ultimately their private devotion and worship to the Lord. What grieves my heart in it all is that such individuals seemed to have lost *the simplicity of devotion to Christ*. Anyone who becomes singularly invested in such pet doctrines loses sight of the fact that whatever perceived victory they may obtain, through their arguments with others, is ultimately a meaningless one which undermines Christ's true glory, and all of this offers no real edification to anyone. When the dust of all such debating settles, nothing is left but an atonement that is robbed of its true glory, and a people who have forgotten *the true Victor in it all*. Therefore, many in the church today despair greatly - like John who wept because he had forgotten the victory of Christ. To lose sight of Christ's promised victory brings only sadness and hopelessness; it robs the church of her vitality, joy, and enthusiasm for Christ and the Gospel's worldwide mission. In many ways, the modern church is drowning in the *slough* of Revelation 5:4[115] rather than rejoicing with the host of heaven in the Song of the Victorious Lamb of God (Revelation 5:5-10). Therefore, the church must forsake such a dreadful path and embrace the better examples of worship given to us in Scripture. Like Mary, we must return to the simplicity of devotion to Christ, being at the Savior's feet and hearing from Him. Like John, we must call to mind the victory of our Savior so that we might *turn from sorrow to joy in view of the Conqueror – the Lord Jesus Christ*. A great part of this restoration must include a return to the vast

---

[115] Revelation 5:4 And I began to weep greatly, because no one was found worthy to open the book, or to look into it;

treasure of Christ's victorious atonement, because His victory of the cross is the master gem in His kingly crown. When the church looks to Christ, to the wonder of His victory, as well as to the riches of His kingdom, then she is lifted up to greater praise and empowered service. This is true because the doctrine of the atonement offers many applications for the disciples of Jesus Christ, even beyond the most important application of all: *our redemption*. Thus, the doctrine of the atonement does not only instruct us about *what Christ did*, but it also teaches us about *how we should live* in view of His loving servitude and sacrifice. Great is the bounty of practical truth that flows from the treasure chest of Christ's loving example! In all its riches, we see many important truths, but our focus in this section will be set upon following the example of Christ's sacrificial love as it relates to: *1. Our daily motivation in life, 2. A husband's love for his wife, 3. A wife's love for her husband, 4. Our conduct in this world, 5. Our love for the brethren and 6. Our joy in evangelism.* Let's begin by looking at the atonement's impact on the Christian's genuine motivation for daily living, as we are called to walk in love after the pattern of Christ Himself.

THE GREATEST OF THESE IS LOVE
If I ...do not have love, I am nothing
1 Corinthians 13:2

How important it is to understand that the Lord desires worship that is genuine, for the sacrifices of God are a broken spirit and a contrite heart.[116] When we study this point carefully, we are then led to consider the very nature of the Christian's right motivation when rendering obedience to the Lord. Such a query regarding

---

[116] 1 Samuel 15:22-23; Psalm 51:17 The sacrifices of God are a broken spirit; A broken and a contrite heart, O God, Thou wilt not despise.

motivation has received a great deal of attention in recent years. Depending on what pundit one may listen to, the proposed motives often range anywhere from fear to personal joy or experiential knowledge. The amount of ink and paper being spent on this topic is extraordinary and causes one to wonder if there really ought to be such a divergence of opinion. For example, some have suggested that joy (*chairō*) is the *sine qua non* of a Christian's proper motivation. In this view, the worshipper's subjective experience of joy represents the ultimate foundation for service and worship. Still others have placed the same emphasis on the experiential knowledge of God (*epignōskō*);[117] or others upon one's subjective desire for Him (*epithumia*);[118] and even the fear of God (*phobos*) is suggested as the Christian's main source of motivation.[119] Ultimately, every one of these aspects of worship *is important*, but none of them *singularly establishes the Christian's central motivation for living.* Our joy in Him, knowledge of Him, desire for Him, and godly fear before Him, are all important components of Christian living; however, when any one of these is emphasized disproportionately, an imbalance is thus created. Like individual spokes of a wheel, *one alone will not do.* But there *is* an important hub to this wheel of Christian living; one that connects the spokes of joy, knowledge, desire and godly fear – it is the love of God (*agape*).[120] Without such a hub, you have no wheel; or as the Apostle Paul said: "if I... do not have love, I am nothing." Parenthetically, let me say that it is extremely important that believers *only* emphasize what the *Scriptures emphasize*, while being very careful with the words that are used from the Bible. You see, most theological errors begin, not with some obvious or

---

[117] Colossians 1:6.
[118] Philippians 1:23.
[119] 1 Peter 2:17, Philippians 2:12.
[120] 1 John 4:19 We love, because He first loved us.

intended error, but with the slightest misrepresentations of the Word. Sometimes these errors are even advanced with the best of intentions by well meaning people. Overall, there is great safety and spiritual profit to be found when one emphasizes what the Scriptures themselves emphasize. With this in view, let us look to the Savior and learn from Him concerning this important subject of Christian motivation. When the Lord was asked about which commandment was the greatest of them all, His response established the preeminence of God-centered love:

> Matthew 22:36-40: 36 *"Teacher, which is the great commandment in the Law?" 37 And He said to him, "'You shall love the Lord your God with all your heart, and with all your soul, and with all your mind.' 38 "This is the great and foremost commandment. 39 "The second is like it, 'You shall love your neighbor as yourself.' 40 "On these two commandments depend the whole Law and the Prophets."*

Out of all the law and the prophets, our Lord could have chosen any number of summary commands that would inform us about the central motivation for Christian life and servitude. After all, the Old Testament is teaming with expressions of great joy towards God (*samah*);[121] the importance of a personal knowledge of Him (*yada'*);[122] the believer's subjective desire for Him (*'anag*);[123] even reverence before Him (*yir'ah*);[124] and yet Christ singled out just one, central hub of Christian devotion: *the love of God ('ahab)*.[125] Of all that Christ could have emphasized, He chose to herald the greatest of them all - *theocentric (God-centered) love*. What makes Matthew 22:36-40 so strikingly beautiful is that the Lord's message

---

[121] Psalm 32:11.
[122] Psalm 100:3.
[123] Psalm 37:4.
[124] Psalm 19:9.
[125] Deuteronomy 6:4-5.

is given with absolutely perfect representation; that is, Christ was the greatest preacher of all, not only because of His oratory skill, but also because He was an infallible manifestation of the truth that He proclaimed. Thus, this priority of *theocentric love* was proclaimed with perfect representation, through the One who said:

> *John 14:31 but the world must learn that I love the Father and that I do exactly what my Father has commanded me. [NIV]*

We examined this verse when we considered the *God centered intent of the cross,* in chapter 2. There we learned that Christ's atonement, on our behalf, had at its center this motive of godly love; ultimately, *all that Christ did was secured by His love for the Father.* Therefore this centrality of love is key, for it reminds us that the Christian possesses a special *union* with the Lord that is grounded in a *loving relationship.* Therefore, for the Disciples of Christ, the motives of joy, knowledge, desire, and godly fear are all linked to this central relationship of love for God. So important is this, that without it we would be reduced to a heartless pursuit of self. But in light of our relationship to God as children, we are to walk in such a manner as to *seek His good pleasure*:

> *Ephesians 5:1-2, 8 & 10: 1 Therefore be imitators of God, as beloved children; 2 and walk in love, just as Christ also loved you, and gave Himself up for us, an offering and a sacrifice to God as a fragrant aroma ... 8 for you were formerly darkness, but now you are light in the Lord; walk as children of light ... 10 trying to learn what is pleasing to the Lord.*

As the children of God, who have been enveloped in His perfect love, we are called to *imitate Him by walking in love.* As His beloved children, we have this unspeakable privilege of walking in such a manner so as to *learn what is pleasing to the Lord.* For those who truly love the Lord, this pursuit of *His pleasure* will establish within them a true joy, desire, knowledge, godly reverence and, overall, a deeper love for Him.[126] Here is the Christian's *true motive for daily life*, patterned after the perfect Son of God who loved the Father and offered up His life as a sacrifice out of obedience to Him - *for He always did the things that were pleasing to the Father*.[127] The Lamb's loving obedience to the Father, the summit of which was the cross upon which He died, stands as the highest, most precious, and majestic example of all. Let us therefore *follow Him*[128] and walk in love as we learn what is pleasing to the Lord!

THE EXCEPTIONAL LOVE OF A HUSBAND
Husbands, love your wives, just as Christ also loved the church and gave Himself up for her;
Ephesians 5:25

When Christ offered Himself as a sacrifice for our sin, He gave the greatest example of *theocentric love ever displayed*. Our Lord's service of love to the Father therefore stands at the heart of every aspect of Christian living. Especially for husbands, Christ's example of love is a strong reminder that no husband can love his wife well if he doesn't love the Lord first. Therefore, Christ gives us the greatest measure of love within any marriage union; and by this example, the spiritual man must understand that *he is to love his wife as an outflow of his love for God*. Such a theocentric priority will make the Lord his passionate priority before any other.[129] The union of marriage must be understood with this priority of love – The husband is not to place his wife above all, rather, the Lord is

---

[126] John 14:21.
[127] John 8:29 And He who sent Me is with Me; He has not left Me alone, for I always do the things that are pleasing to Him.
[128] John 21:22 Jesus *said to him, "If I want him to remain until I come, what is that to you? You follow Me!"
[129] John 2:13-17.

his highest priority. Such a priority does not demean the wife, nor lessen the quality of love that the husband has for her. On the contrary, this is the highest quality of love that he can offer to her – *the godly love of Christ*. The implications of this concept of love are vast. The imitation of Christ takes on some wonderful connotations with this simple observation. As Christ cherished the church as a gift from the Father, so too is the spiritual man to love his bride as a gift from God. In imitating Christ, the spiritual husband will grow in his desire, compassion, and faithfulness towards his wife. The true believer holds dearly to the endowments of the Lord because of his deep love for the Giver:

> *James 1:17 Every good thing bestowed and every perfect gift is from above, coming down from the Father of lights, with whom there is no variation, or shifting shadow.*

By this principle it is understood that the spirit-filled man will have a passionate desire for his wife because she is a wonderful and special gift from God Himself.[130] Therefore, the husband's valuation of His wife is not based upon her performance, physical beauty, or skill at cooking; rather it is based upon the gracious provision of the Lord who gave her: Proverbs 18:22 "He who finds a wife finds a good thing, And obtains favor from the Lord." The spiritual husband is to love his wife in a multifaceted way, but his love for her must be God-centered such that he cherishes her *in the Lord*. Christ alone provides the valid measure for true manliness and godly leadership. Leadership that is patterned after the Savior's love will nurture peace, joy, and growth to the family of God. Such leadership within the family, which edifies and builds others up, requires constant vigilance, and labor in the Spirit, as one follows the loving example of the Bridegroom of the church.

---

[130] Gen. 2:23.

THE EXCEPTIONAL LOVE OF A WIFE
*In the same way, you wives, be submissive
to your own husbands
1 Peter 3:1*

The subject of *submission to authority* is not a very popular one today. The American spirit is often riddled with unbiblical concepts concerning freedom and responsibility. Unbeknownst to many in this land, true freedom is not found in the ability to do whatever one wants, rather, it is found in serving the Lord as a bondservant:

> *1 Peter 2:16 Act as free men, and do not use your freedom as a covering for evil, but use it as bondslaves of God.*

For many, this isn't the American way; but at least it is Christ's way. It is an amazing thought to consider, that the most powerful human being who ever walked the face of this planet, walked as a humble servant - *even unto His own death*. Christ submitted to the Father's will, a will *which included His being subject to the dictates of the wicked men who crucified Him;*[131] and at the center of it all was His theocentric love which led Him to the cross to die in our stead. 1 Peter 2:16 has an important context. At the broadest level that context was one of persecution and suffering,[132] such that Peter wrote to his audience in order to encourage them to persevere in the midst of a cold and wicked world. In order to do this, Peter presented the master gem of Christ's sacrifice as the greatest example of godly, humble submission:

---

[131] Acts 2:23 this Man, delivered up by the predetermined plan and foreknowledge of God, you nailed to a cross by the hands of godless men and put Him to death.
[132] 1 Peter 1:16-17.

1 Peter 2:21-23: 21 For you have been called for this purpose, since Christ also suffered for you, leaving you an example for you to follow in His steps, 22 who committed no sin, nor was any deceit found in His mouth; 23 and while being reviled, He did not revile in return; while suffering, He uttered no threats, but kept entrusting Himself to Him who judges righteously;

From chapters 2 to 3, Peter exhorts believers to consider carefully their conduct in the midst of their wicked world. At the center of this section stands this example of Christ's perfect submission to the Father. Christ's own example of loving and humble servitude is that which Peter draws from when he calls upon believers to submit to their imperfect authorities in this life. Four times in this section Peter speaks of the godly Christian's humble *submission* (*hupotagēte*: 1 Peter 2:13, 18; 3:1, 5) to authority. While these relationships are all different, they still share the common denominator of Christ-like submission. Ultimately, submission, humility, gentleness, and reverence are qualities that are heralded as the crucial Christ-like imitations which establish a godly testimony before men. It is in this very context of Christ-like imitation that Peter enjoined wives to submit to their own husbands. Peter instructed wives to submit *in the same way;*[133] that is, after the same pattern of godly submission for all Christians, whose ultimate pattern is Christ Himself (1 Peter 2:21-25). Peter's audience at that time was most needful of these instructions in light of the fact that his epistle was most likely written during the 9th year of the reign of Emperor Nero. It would only be a year later that the Neronian persecution of the church would commence on a large scale. Prior to this (A.D. 64), the church had already become a

---

[133] G. *'omoiōs* – In the same way or in like manner. "'In the same way' (*omoiōs*) implies that the paragraph is another in a series devoted to the subject of Christian submission." D. Edmond Hiebert, 1 Peter, (BMH BOOKS, Winona Lake, Indiana), p. 195.

cultural outcast and was often the subject of rejection, ridicule, and scattered persecutions. As well, in the 1st century Roman world, the legal freedoms of wives were much more limited than in our day. The Roman doctrine of *patria potestas* greatly limited the rights and freedoms of the wife.[134] These civil standards would change within a half century, but to his immediate readers the reality of suffering under harsh conditions was quite real.[135] But Peter exhorted them to remain faithful to the Lord despite the standards of Roman law and government. In so doing, Peter encouraged wives to look to the example of Sarah who obeyed without fear:

> 1 Peter 3:6 ...Sarah obeyed Abraham, calling him lord, and you have become her children if you do what is right without being frightened by any fear.

Submitting to imperfect leadership can be, humanly speaking, a fearful prospect, whether to an ungodly king, ruler, or husband; but the woman who fears God will submit to her husband as an expression of *exceptional love for the Lord Himself*. Such submission is itself a testimony of grace in the home that communicates the glory of Christ, *much louder than words*.

---

[134] Shelton, As The Romans Did, p. 278.

[135] Will Durant affirms that Roman law did change during the reign of Emperor Hadrian (A.D. 117-138): "The second person in Roman law was the father...Rule through family and clan diminished as population became more abundant and diverse, and life more mobile, commercial, and complex; kinship, status, and custom were replaced by contract and law. Children won greater freedom from their parents, wives from their husbands, individuals from their groups. Trajan compelled a father to emancipate a son whom he had maltreated; Hadrian took from the father the right of life and death over his household and transferred it to the courts." Will Durant, The Story of Civilization: Part III, *Caesar and Christ* (Simon and Schuster, New York), p. 395.

The Exceptional Love of Heaven's Citizens

Submit yourselves for the Lord's sake to every human
institution, whether to a king
as the one in authority
1 Peter 2:13

Peter's important instructions, in 1 Peter chapters 2 and 3, are not only important for wives (1 Peter 3:1-6), but they are also crucial for all Christians, no matter what their circumstances are. Whether as a citizen under governing authority (2:13-17), or as an employee under the authority of an employer (2:18), all believers are called to look intently at the perfect example of Christ's loving servitude to the Father:

> *1 Peter 2:23 ...and while being reviled, He did not revile in return; while suffering, He uttered no threats, but kept entrusting Himself to Him who judges righteously;*

Christ endured such hostility by sinners against Himself[136] because He continually entrusted Himself *to Him who judges righteously*. In other words, Christ endured the cross because *His focus remained set upon the Father whom He trusted*; the Father whom *He loved and sought to please*. Once again, the theocentric nature of the cross stands as the ultimate example for the Christian's life. In light of His perfect example, believers are to subject themselves to the imperfect authorities in this life, *while entrusting themselves to Him who judges righteously*:

> *1 Peter 2:13-18: 13 Therefore submit yourselves to every ordinance of man for the Lord's sake, whether to the king as supreme, 14 or to governors, as to those who are sent by him for the punishment of evildoers and for the praise of those who do good. 15 For this is the will of God, that*

---

[136] Hebrews 12:3.

> *by doing good you may put to silence the ignorance of foolish men—16 as free, yet not using liberty as a cloak for vice, but as bondservants of God. 17 Honor all people. Love the brotherhood. Fear God. Honor the king. 18 Servants, be submissive to your masters with all fear, not only to the good and gentle, but also to the harsh. [NKJV]*

I have already mentioned the struggles that exist in our American culture regarding authority and submission to authority. I truly believe that Peter's instructions are an important and needful corrective for this generation. Particularly here in our nation, there is a great tendency to presume that America is, or ever was, a completely Christian nation. It is certainly the case that, in our beginning, there were a great number of godly men who loved the Lord and His Word. However, there were many secular and merely religious men who did not know Christ, as it is in our day. But despite this reality, many believers press on in the political forum expecting the citizens of this nation to embrace the standards of God's Word, apart from a transformation of the heart. However, one cannot legislate a real change in the culture where there is no work of the Spirit in the human heart. It is certainly true that we are free, even responsible, to speak out concerning our views within the arena of public opinion and debate; however, we must remember that the people of this world watch our politics very carefully. They want to see if we are just like the masses in this world, or if there is a real difference in us at all. Therefore, the believer's participation in work and politics must always be grounded in a God glorifying submission that is patterned after the example of Jesus Christ. What Peter offers us in these important chapters, is the master gem of Christ's loving servitude to the Father; a servitude that even endured the harsh treatment of a wicked government that led Him to His death. The Savior *suffered for us, leaving us an example, such that we should follow His steps* (2:21). Therefore, *though He was reviled, He did not revile in return*

(2:23). It is only by imitating Christ's humble submission, as ultimately manifested through His death on the cross, that we have any hope of being a viable witness for Him in this world of darkness:

> *1 Peter 2:12 having your conduct honorable among the Gentiles, that when they speak against you as evildoers, they may, by your good works which they observe, glorify God in the day of visitation.*

Believers are free to participate as citizens of this nation, but in all our speech and conduct, we must never forget our singular duty as the citizens of Christ's kingdom:

> *Philippians 1:27 Only let your conduct be worthy of the gospel of Christ, so that whether I come and see you or am absent, I may hear of your affairs, that you stand fast in one spirit, with one mind striving together for the faith of the gospel.*

As we fulfill our earthly citizenship in this life, our highest priority is not found in winning the political battles of men. Rather, the true politics (*conduct ~ politeuesthē*[137]) of believers must comport with the Gospel of Jesus Christ, for *no other standard will do*. The Christian's ultimate citizenship is not of this world, which is passing away, but is heavenly and eternal.[138] Because of this, our earthly citizenry must point others to the kingdom of Christ. Our

---

[137] G. *politeuesthē* – The root concept of this word *polis* (city) establishes the foundational meaning of citizenship. The word politics is derived from this Greek word. In their day, someone who was political was a person who was active as a citizen in his community. However, by modern standards the thought of politics has taken on the more particular thought of formal participation in government. Overall, Paul's point is clear. The believer's citizenry in the world must hold to only one standard: the Gospel of Jesus Christ.

[138] Philippians 3:20 For our citizenship is in heaven, from which we also eagerly wait for the Savior, the Lord Jesus Christ,

interaction with the world must always be rooted in a Christ-centered love so that when unbelievers watch and hear us, whether in the political forum or in the workplace, their conclusion should be that *we love the Lord our God with all our heart, with all our soul and with all our strength*!

THE EXCEPTIONAL LOVE OF THE BRETHREN

*Greater love has no one than this,
than to lay down one's life
for his friends.
John 15:13*

One of the most profound errors of doctrine to be found within the modern church has to do with the doctrine of the love of God. As we have already assessed, the Father has an exceptional love for His Son; and the Son has this same love for His Father. As well, the Lord has an exceptional love for His people as they are called His sheep; His bride; the Father's children; and Christ's friends. In the case of Ephesians chapter 5, we saw that Paul called the church Christ's bride in view of the heavenly wedding to come.[139] The simplicity of this image reminds us that Christ did not have many brides in His loving view, rather just one; the one whom the Father gave to Him from before the foundation of the world.[140] Such a beautiful picture of Christ's *loving fidelity* has its important application for men and their wives. A husband does not love all women as he does his wife – may it never be! His love is not spread out *universally* and *indiscriminately*; rather it is focused *uniquely* upon his one and only wife. It should be obvious that the conclusion of *universalism* poses a strange risk to many other teachings in the Scriptures if one carries the theological reasoning

---

[139] Revelation 19:7-10, Ephesians 5:25.
[140] Ephesians 1:3-6,

of universalism to its end. One area where such a risk has proven to be problematic is found within the dynamic of the Christian assembly. For years the doctrine of God's *exceptional love* has been systematically replaced with a kind of *unexceptional love;* one which makes little to no distinction between the sheep and the goats. Because of this, many in the church today see no problem with receiving the world into its own ranks. If the Lord's love is so *unexceptional*, then why make any distinction at all? With an ecclesiology such as this, the new paradigm focuses on doing all that is necessary to enfold all men without exception, regardless of their Gospel convictions. The choral chant of such "churches" has become "*just as I am without one plea*" in the worst possible sense. Theological standards such as these leave the sinner without any call to repentance over sin; after all, they are welcome *just as they are.* Within the morass of this confounding message, the gem of God's *exceptional love* is absolutely lost. The end result is that the church's relationship with the world is confused; the purity of Christian fellowship is thus corrupted; the message of mankind's enmity with God is forsaken; and resultantly, the Gospel message becomes a mere upgrade for people who would like to add a form of Christianity to their busy, idolatrous lives.

What is the Christian's relationship to other believers? What should it be with the unbeliever? If these questions are not addressed carefully, the result could render horrific results for the body of Christ. So first, let us consider the exceptional love of the brethren.

> *John 15:12-14: 12 This is My commandment, that you love one another as I have loved you. 13 Greater love has no one than this, than to lay down one's life for his friends. 14 You are My friends if you do whatever I command you. [NKJV]*

Christ's loving example, set through His atoning work on the cross, provides the standard for the exceptional love which binds the saints together as *the family of God*.

> *Romans 12:10 Be devoted to one another in brotherly love; give preference to one another in honor;*

Love is the very bond of Christian fellowship[141] and it is the precious foundation of filial affection among Christ's brethren; and as we observed earlier, Christ's love for His own is unique[142] since it is patterned after the special love of the Father for the Son:

> *John 15:9 As the Father loved Me, I also have loved you; abide in My love. [NKJV]*

Thus, the very love that has been bestowed upon the people of God's choosing[143] is the same love that knits us together as the *unique children of God*. Therefore, it is by this *exceptional love* that all men will know that we are Christ's disciples.[144] However, a common misconception today is that this doctrine of exceptional love then nullifies the church's love for the lost, or, for that matter, God's universal love for the world. This simply is not the case. This then leads us to the important question regarding the believer's relationship with the lost of this world. Simply put, we are to love

---

[141] Colossians 3:14 But above all these things put on love, which is the bond of perfection.

[142] John 13:1 Now before the feast of the Passover, when Jesus knew that His hour had come that He should depart from this world to the Father, having loved His own who were in the world, He loved them to the end.

[143] 1 John 4:19.

[144] John 13:35 By this all men will know that you are My disciples, if you have love for one another.

them as our Father loves them. This merciful love, which God has for all men, is a love of patience, mercy, and longsuffering.

> *Psalm 103:8-10: 8 The Lord is merciful and gracious, Slow to anger, and abounding in mercy. 9 He will not always strive with us, nor will He keep His anger forever. 10 He has not dealt with us according to our sins, nor punished us according to our iniquities.*

The proof of his mercy, signified by the rainbow,[145] is evidenced by the fact that sinful men are granted the privileges of life, having the daily opportunity to enjoy the world which God created. But this *beneficent and merciful* love is certainly not the same as His *exceptional love* for His own. God's love is not monochromatic such that it is the same for everyone, as we saw in the example of Jacob and Esau. Therefore, the children of God are to imitate their heavenly Father by extending an *exceptional love* for the brethren, while manifesting a *compassionate love* to those who are our enemies, just as the Lord extends a compassionate love to those who are at enmity with Him.[146] In this latter case, the Lord's example of *patient, merciful, and compassionate love* provides the important foundation for the manner in which the believer is to extend the Gospel to others. With patience, mercy, and compassion, our invitation to the world is one whereby we call them to enter into an *exceptional love relationship* with the Lord, which is the privileged relationship of *sonship* through faith in the Lord Jesus Christ. We must mercifully remind them that the love which they presently receive, displays the goodness and mercy of God, however, their continued rejection of such mercy will only

---

[145] Genesis 9:14-15: 14 "It shall be, when I bring a cloud over the earth, that the rainbow shall be seen in the cloud; 15 "and I will remember My covenant which is between Me and you and every living creature of all flesh; the waters shall never again become a flood to destroy all flesh.
[146] Matthew 5:44-45.

compound their final judgment before Christ, whom they have forsaken.[147] Thus, the believer's relationship with the world is predicated upon one very important relationship: *the compassionate Gospel call*. However, the believer's relationship with Christ's sheep is a unique one that is based upon *filial love*. It is a special relationship since it is rooted and grounded in the *exceptional love of Christ*. Therefore, while we are to love all men, we must do so especially with those who are of the household of faith:

> *Galatians 6:10 Therefore, as we have opportunity, let us do good to all, especially to those who are of the household of faith.*

The church is the household of God, containing His redeemed children. It is not to be a place that gives preference to the unbeliever, but to believers;[148] therefore, instead of transforming the church so that it might become more appealing to the world (in the name of evangelism) the church is directed to take its evangelism out into the world.[149] Many in our day have endeavored to make the church more worldly with the false hope of increasing their Gospel witness; however, the opposite effect has dominated. Because the church has imported such worldliness into its halls of worship, the Gospel message has become weakened, and with this, the Christian's responsibility to pursue the world with the truth is confused:

> *John 17:16-18: 16 They are not of the world, even as I am not of the world. 17 Sanctify them in the truth; Thy word is truth. 18 As Thou didst send Me into the world, I also have sent them into the world.*

---

[147] Romans 1:18-20.

[148] Romans 12:10 Be kindly affectionate to one another with brotherly love, in honor giving preference to one another;

[149] John 17:18.

The children of God must give priority to the building up of the body of Christ through corporate worship that honors Christ – not the world. The sheep of Christ must be sanctified in truth and nothing else. And as Christ's disciples grow and mature we are to *go out into the world* with the Gospel, in view of the pattern and petitions of our Savior.

THE EXCEPTIONAL LOVE OF GOD'S MESSENGERS

Therefore I endure all things for the sake of the elect, that they also may obtain the salvation which is in Christ Jesus with eternal glory.
2 Timothy 2:10

Of all the contentions ever raised on behalf of universal atonement, the argument of *Gospel motivation* is perhaps the most divisive one of them all. The line of reasoning in this argument usually includes accusations of a disingenuous Gospel message: after all, if God has foreordained that not all should be saved, then the Gospel messenger cannot *genuinely* offer the Gospel call to *all men without exception*. But such thinking is the product of human reasoning, as discussed earlier. While there are other facets of this poor line of thought, we will address the core charge of a *disingenuous Gospel ministry*. Once again, we can only calibrate our thinking by going to the Word of God on this important matter. By looking at the example and teaching of the Apostle Paul, we can better understand if such a charge has any credibility to it, or not. Remember, it was Paul who taught us that *it does not depend upon him who wills, or him who runs, but upon God who has mercy – for the Lord will have mercy on whom He desires and He will harden whom He desires*. How did this immovable doctrine of God's absolute sovereignty effect Paul's motivation to proclaim the

Gospel? Answer: *wonderfully!* When Paul wrote his second epistle to Timothy he prefaced his letter with a reminder concerning the nature of our salvation:

> *2 Timothy 1:8-9: 8 Therefore do not be ashamed of the testimony of our Lord, or of me His prisoner; but join with me in suffering for the gospel according to the power of God, 9 who has saved us, and called us with a holy calling, not according to our works, but according to His own purpose and grace which was granted us in Christ Jesus from all eternity,*

Paul was offering Timothy a very important anchor for the soul. It is the anchor which is grounded in God's sovereign grace and immutable promises, for it was *according to God's purpose and grace* that any are saved; and His gift of salvation was *granted in Christ Jesus from all eternity.* What else does an intimidated soldier need to hear but that his Commander in chief will never leave him or forsake him, but will keep him until the end! God is faithful to bring those whom He chose *from all eternity, according to His gracious purpose and choice,* to saving faith and to final glory. Timid Timothy needed such a reminder so that he might endure the hardships which faced him in the ministry. For Paul, and for Timothy, the doctrine of God's absolute sovereignty provided a very practical hope; one that brings about endurance in the believer. Rather than destroying their motivation, the truth of God's sovereignty supplied an important impetus to press on in what was a very difficult battle of faith.[150] But Paul's encouragements to Timothy did not end in chapter 1. In chapter 2 he offered to Timothy a very important piece of instruction that would help him to remain motivated in his Gospel ministry, if even in the face of horrific opposition:

---

[150] 2 Timothy 4:7-18.

> 2 Timothy 2:8-9: 8 Remember Jesus Christ, risen from the dead, descendant of David, according to my gospel, 9 for which I suffer hardship even to imprisonment as a criminal; but the word of God is not imprisoned.

Paul was being treated as a criminal for preaching the Gospel of Jesus Christ and yet he was able to endure it all. He rejoiced because even though he was imprisoned, the Word of God was not! As we see in his epistle to the Philippians, Paul understood God's sovereign purposes, even in his imprisonments.[151] The Apostle comprehended that the Lord was spreading the Gospel, through him, and bringing many to faith in the city of Rome and ultimately, within Caesar's own household.[152] God's sovereign work and purposes made it so that he could rejoice greatly, rather than despair.[153] But what Paul said next in 2 Timothy 2:10 is even more profound as it relates to *God's sovereignty and our labor of evangelism*:

> 2 Timothy 2:10: 10 For this reason I endure all things for the sake of those who are chosen, that they also may obtain the salvation which is in Christ Jesus and with it eternal glory.

Paul clearly tells us here that he endured all his sufferings for the sake of *those who are chosen!* Paul uses here the word *chosen* or *elect*, the root of which is *eklektos*. This same word was used by Peter to speak of Christ as being *choice and precious in the sight of*

---

[151] Philippians 1:12-14: 12 Now I want you to know, brethren, that my circumstances have turned out for the greater progress of the gospel, 13 so that my imprisonment in the cause of Christ has become well known throughout the whole praetorian guard and to everyone else, 14 and that most of the brethren, trusting in the Lord because of my imprisonment, have far more courage to speak the word of God without fear.
[152] Philippians 4:22 All the saints greet you, especially those of Caesar's household.
[153] Philippians 1:3-4, 18, 2:18, 3:1, 4:4.

God;[154] and a similar form is used in Ephesians 1:4 which tells us that God *chose us in Him before the foundation of the world.* Very simply, plainly, *and significantly* – Paul endured great hostility in his Gospel ministry *for the sake of God's elect, that they may obtain the salvation which is in Christ Jesus and with it eternal glory.* Dr. Owen gives us some important thoughts on this matter:

> *"The ministers of the Gospel, who are stewards of the mysteries of Christ, and to whom the word of reconciliation is committed, being acquainted only with revealed things (the Lord lodging His purposes and intentions towards particular persons in the secret ark of his own bosom, not to be pryed into), are bound to admonish all, and warn all men, to whom they are sent; giving the same commands, proposing the same promises, making tenders of Jesus Christ in the same manner, to all, that the elect, whom they know not but by the event, may obtain, whilst the rest are hardened."*[155]

The doctrine of God's absolute sovereignty did not dampen Paul's enthusiasm for preaching, rather *it upheld it entirely.* Paul understood that as he proclaimed the Gospel, those who were Christ's elect sheep would hear the Savior and believe unto salvation. Like Lydia, who was given the gift of faith[156] such that her heart was opened to receive the things spoken by Paul, so too will all of Christ's sheep hear the voice of the Good shepherd and obtain the very salvation that was granted to them in Christ Jesus from all eternity. Such knowledge did not quiet Paul's spirit; instead it further inflamed him to proclaim the powerful Gospel, trusting that God would accomplish the work of Salvation. The very Apostle who declared, in Romans 9, that the Lord will *have mercy on whom*

---

[154] 1 Peter 2:4-6.
[155] Owen, The Death of Death, p. 313.
[156] Philippians 1:29.

He desires and will harden whom He desires, is the same man who said:

> Romans 9:1-3: 1 *I am telling the truth in Christ, I am not lying, my conscience bearing me witness in the Holy Spirit, 2 that I have great sorrow and unceasing grief in my heart. 3 For I could wish that I myself were accursed, separated from Christ for the sake of my brethren, my kinsmen according to the flesh,*

Paul understood that only the Lord knows who are His.[157] He also knew that salvation depended upon God's sovereign choice and not the efforts of man; and yet Paul *was in no way silent, or dispassionate, concerning his hunger for the lost to be saved*. The doctrine of God's *gracious* election gave him a confidence that *there would be an abundant harvest of souls,* and Paul knew that he could trust the Lord for the outcome. Thus, he knew that what was a secret to him (the number of the elect), presented no secret or *contingency* to the Lord. For the child of God, such ignorance is a blessing, and leaves us with the great privilege of broadcasting the Gospel to all flesh, indiscriminately *and passionately*; therefore, when the Philippian jailer came and inquired "what must I do to be saved?" the Apostolic response was not: "are you elect?" This would be the product of foolish, human reasoning. Rather, the Apostle's passionate reply was delivered, imperatively: "Believe! In the Lord Jesus Christ and you will be saved." Because of his God-centered confidence, *and exceptional love for Christ,* Paul could simply discharge the Gospel of Christ and leave the redemptive results to Him. The foundation of God's absolute sovereignty helped Paul remember that while he was an instrumental soldier for the Gospel, it is the Lord *alone* who is the sovereign Captain of our salvation.

---

[157] 2 Timothy 2:19.

Following The Victorious Lamb

The things you have learned and received and heard
and seen in me, practice these things;
and the God of peace
shall be with you.
Philippians 4:9

To the extent that today's church lacks the peace and rest of God, it does so because of the lack of simple devotion to the principles of Scripture. Paul made a profound promise at the end of his epistle to the church at Philippi; it was a promise of peace to those who would *practice what he taught them*. And what did Paul teach in his letter to the Philippians? He taught them (and us) that the believer can joyfully[158] maintain the unity[159] of the church by looking intently at Christ's loving sacrifice on the cross. In a sense, Paul taught the Philippians that the doctrine of Christ's atoning *sacrifice* has deep and practical implications concerning the very nature of the church's fellowship, life, and ministry. Apart from grace, and without Christ's example, all that we are left with is our own selfishness, insincerity, and deep despair. Putting it another way, a joyless and divisive church is one that has lost its vision *of Christ's humble servitude and victorious atonement*. His humility, and resultant victory, is the basis for His future exaltation and it is also, therefore, the foundation of the believer's joy:

> *Philippians 2:5-11: 5 Let this mind be in you which was also in Christ Jesus, 6 who, being in the form of God, did not consider it robbery to be equal with God, 7 but made Himself of no reputation, taking the form of a bondservant, and coming in the likeness of men. 8 And being found in appearance as a man, He humbled Himself and became obedient to the point of death, even the death of the cross. 9 Therefore God also has*

---

[158] Philippians 1:4, 25; 2:2, 17, 18, 29; 3:1; 4:1, 4, 10.
[159] Philippians 2.

highly exalted Him and given Him the name which is above every name, 10 that at the name of Jesus every knee should bow, of those in heaven, and of those on earth, and of those under the earth, 11 and that every tongue should confess that Jesus Christ is Lord, to the glory of God the Father.

We have a great need to apply, continually, the doctrine of Christ's sacrificial atonement by *trusting in His perfect work* and by *imitating His humility and love in everything*. Those who believe in Him are now gloriously covered with His righteousness;[160] their hope and confidence lies not in the deeds that they do, but in the single deed of righteousness that was accomplished by Christ on the cross through His unspeakable humility and great love for the Father. All in all, His victorious propitiation *and His godly example,* provide the believer with real joy and hope. By His finished work and loving example, the true believer possesses the peace of God, rather than the temporal peace of this world; and as believers manifest Christ's humility, joy, and peace in this world, they will appear as lights in the midst of a crooked and perverse generation.

May the church be further empowered to display His glory in the presence of this lost and dying world![161]

---

[160] Galatians 3:24-27.
[161] Titus 3:5, Philippians 2:14-15.

ALL NATIONS UNDER GOD

CHRIST'S TRIUMPH OVER TRADITION

CHRIST'S TRIUMPH OVER TRADITION

You nicely set aside the commandment of God in order to keep your tradition.
Mark 7:9

When Christ walked the earth, Judaism had become a dead and soulless machine. Many of the religious leaders searched the Scriptures as an academic exercise, but without the love of God in their hearts.[162] We see this illustrated clearly since our Lord's ministry was often met with harsh opposition by those who were supposed to be the greatest spiritual leaders in the land. This is even evident from the very beginning of our Lord's ministry. When Christ began His ministry in Nazareth, He entered the synagogue there and read from the scroll of Isaiah. We are told that at that moment, all who heard Him spoke well of Him.[163] But then the Savior did something that wasn't expected. He proceeded to tell His listeners that in the days of Elijah, the Lord bypassed all the widows of Israel and sent His servant to only one in Zarephath of Sidon. He then taught them that in the days of Elisha there were many lepers in Israel, and yet the Lord sent His servant to only one: Naaman of Syria. As a result of His teaching, those who originally spoke well of Him *tried to kill Him*! Yes, those who were there tried to kill Christ by throwing Him *off of a cliff*! What was once an amiable crowd became violently hostile in the face of Christ's teaching about *the absolute sovereignty of God in salvation*. By the standards of Jewish tradition, the Lord's teaching seemed contradictory and vile. To them it was blasphemous to suggest that God would extend His grace to *mere Gentiles* and *not at all to the inhabitants of Israel*. Teaching such as this conflicted with Jewish traditions - *traditions which fostered contempt for the Gentiles*:

---

[162] John 5:39-47.
[163] Luke 4:22.

> *Three things cause a person to transgress against his conscience and the will of his Maker, viz. Gentiles, an evil spirit and the pressing needs caused by poverty. (Erub. 41b)*[164]

Traditions such as these made the evangelism of the Pharisees *self serving,*[165] extremely limited, and grossly prejudicial. Because Christ's teaching on God's sovereignty didn't fit within the paradigm of their traditions, they proceeded to drag Christ to the edge of a cliff in order to end His life. However, there was one problem: *by God's sovereign decree, it wasn't His time to die*! Such a portrait of pugnacity should horrify anyone, and send fear to all our hearts lest we too be guilty of crying out to the Potter: "why have you made me this way?" Had these men possessed hearts that were touched by grace, then their response would have been one of humility rather than pride. Their cry would have been: "Lord, what must I do to be saved?" But sadly, these religious zealots had been nurturing their souls with Pharisaic traditions, rather than the Word of God. This was the unfortunate pattern of life for many in their day, and we should be warned by their example.

THE TRAUMA OF TRADITION
A sword comes into the world because of those
who teach the Torah not in accord
with Tradition.
Abot 5:8

The Pharisees of Christ's day believed strongly in the value of their traditions. This was especially evident because they taught that

---

[164] Abraham Cohen, Everyman's Talmud, *The Major Teachings of the Rabbinic Sages* (Shocken Books, New York), p. 260.

[165] Matthew 23:15 Woe to you, scribes and Pharisees, hypocrites, because you travel about on sea and land to make one proselyte; and when he becomes one, you make him twice as much a son of hell as yourselves.

those who did not adhere to their traditions[166] would "have no share in the world to come."[167] Even with a peculiar irony, they taught that the sword of violence comes into the world because of those who teach the Torah *apart from tradition*. In reality, violence did erupt frequently when Jewish tradition was opposed, *but only by the Pharisaical guardians of those traditions*. This is the repeated pattern seen in the Gospels. Time and time again, when Christ spoke out against the oral traditions of the Pharisees, He was met with extreme hatred and violence. Clearly, the problem was not with Christ, but with those men who loved their traditions more than God and His Word. In mentioning this, we should be reminded that there is *nothing new under the sun*. The patterns of human depravity find their repeated expressions, generation after generation. We should also be reminded that the true fight of every generation is to resolve to walk by grace *alone*, through faith *alone*, in Christ *alone*, established in the Scriptures *alone* for the glory of God *alone*. These five *solas* of the Reformation represent the very ancient battle of all believers that extends back to the beginning of human history itself;[168] and these same battle cries must be established for every generation, lest we degrade to clichés, rumors, creedalism – *the traditions of men*.

I believe that the modern church is in need of another reformation. The bride of Christ needs desperately to shed the garments of *traditional "Christianity"* and be adorned with white robe *biblical Christianity*. By *traditional*, I mean that *form of religion* which is governed by the traditions of men, rather than by the Word of God.

---

[166] The use of the word "law" in the Mishnah was used by the Pharisees as that which included all *oral, Rabbinic teachings*. Emil Schürer <u>A History of the Jewish People in the Time of Christ</u> (Hendrickson Publishers), 2nd Division, Vol II, p. 12

[167] *Abot* 3:11 B. Neusner, J. (1996, c1988). The Mishnah : A new translation. New Haven: Yale University Press.

[168] Hebrews 11.

While most people would give affirmation to this thought of *the Scriptures alone*, fewer still understand what this requires. Biblical Christianity requires the absolute, unfeigned rejection of all that stands in the way of God's Word such that if God has not *declared* it, then we must be prepared to *dump* it! Such a radical approach to ministry will require some significant battles and uphill climbing, for in today's church there are many who stand at the entrance of the church with nothing but a feigned defense of the Scriptures. Like the armored men in Interpreter's house, from Bunyan's *Pilgrim's Progress*, their resistance to the Gospel is carried out on the very doorsteps of God's own kingdom! In fact, there are many today, whether knowingly or unknowingly, who are nullifying the Gospel's authority, power, beauty, and centrality by means of the traditions of men. And should you dare to approach these armored men, and resist their traditions at all, then you had better be prepared to draw your sword.[169] What is at stake is the very glory of Christ in the church. It is a worthy and *good* fight.

America's culture of Christianity has inherited a theological system that is voluminously supplied by various traditions from its past and present; and like the traditions of the Pharisees, they often contain a mixture of truth and error. But what is most disturbing is the fact that many of these traditions (*via* sermons, hymns, gospel tracts, and famous sayings etc.), have adopted such a legendary status in our culture that they have become a perceived source of authority, *by themselves*; and woe is the one who would dare suggest that there might be something unbiblical about them! At the end of the day, the real danger is that people would find their authority in these popularized traditions, rather than in the Word of God. It is always disconcerting when someone seems to be unwilling to

---

[169] Matthew 11:12 And from the days of John the Baptist until now the kingdom of heaven suffers violence, and violent men take it by force.

search the Scriptures and instead argue about church history; but where is the final authority for church history if it isn't in the Scriptures alone? Whenever people are more apt to quote a man (*via* sermons, tracts, books etc.), rather than Scripture, there ought to be great concern. Obviously, such resources from men *can be helpful*, however, the plumb line of truth is only found in the Word of God. In the following pages, we will examine some of the traditions that continue to bring great havoc to the bride of Christ. These traditions are not new by any means; in fact, they are all very ancient, having a long legacy throughout history.

The Tradition of Free Will
"We are Abraham's descendants, and have never been in bondage to anyone..." [NKJV]
John 8:33

Men wish to believe that they are free, if even at the expense of the plain and obvious truth. Such was the case with the Jews who proudly declared: *"We have never been in bondage to anyone"* in John 8:33. Really? *They were never in bondage to anyone?* The very Jews who were accosting Christ in John chapter 8 seemed to be lacking some significant knowledge in light of their response. Whether they meant physical or spiritual bondage, these Jewish inquisitors were clearly in error. On the one hand, it is quite obvious that the Jewish nation had been subjugated to the rule of Egypt, Babylon, Assyria, Greece, Syria, and Rome. In this sense, the Jews have known precious little but bondage and subjection. On the other hand, if they meant spiritual freedom, then this too was a gross mistake. In either case, Christ's response clarifies their true spiritual condition in light of their sin:

John 8:34-36: 34 Jesus answered them, "Most assuredly, I say to you, whoever commits sin is a slave of sin. 35 "And a slave does not abide in the house forever, but a son abides forever. 36 "Therefore if the Son makes you free, you shall be free indeed." [NKJV]

It doesn't require much to deduce that since *all have sinned*[170] that *all are slaves of sin*. What Christ declares here is indisputable: all men, in light of their corruption, are the bondslaves of sin. I find that these passages are most helpful in light of the present debate concerning man's condition of sin. Many times over I have heard people confidently assert that men have *free will*. To them it is as plain as the nose on their face: "everybody knows that we have free will!" is the traditional cry that I hear. It sounds a great deal like these Jews who did not hesitate for a moment to insist that they were never in bondage to anyone! The partial truth is that men are free – *that is, free like a slave*. A slave who is confined to chains or to a prison cell will have the *freedom* to roam about according to the constraint set by *what binds him* (his chains or his cell). He can proudly declare that he has freedom, but in the end he is a slave who is confined to his bondage. This is the very picture of mankind. Men are *bound, confined,* and *imprisoned* by the constraints of their own sinful nature. They roam about indeed, but they do so in what is called a march of spiritual death:

> *Ephesians 2:1-3: 1 And you were dead in your trespasses and sins, 2 in which you formerly walked according to the course of this world, according to the prince of the power of the air, of the spirit that is now working in the sons of disobedience. 3 Among them we too all formerly lived in the lusts of our flesh, indulging the desires of the flesh and of the mind, and were by nature children of wrath, even as the rest.*

The unbeliever *freely* marches about in this world *as the spiritually dead bondslave of sin*. This he will do until the God of love and

---

[170] Romans 3:23.

mercy[171] imparts life to him. Until then, he remains in this horrific state of death and bondage. Because the unbeliever is spiritually dead, he has not the power to come to Christ apart from the Father's drawing and gift:

> *John 6:44, 65: 44 No one can come to Me, unless the Father who sent Me draws him; and I will raise him up on the last day....65 And He was saying, For this reason I have said to you, that no one can come to Me, unless it has been granted him from the Father.*[172]

The act of a sinner coming to Christ is the work and gift of God the Father. And why is this so? Because men are the spiritually dead bondslaves of sin. Their "freedom" is limited to the nature of their spiritual imprisonment. Without a work of grace and mercy, all of mankind would be lost forever as the children of wrath.

The Tradition of Hypercalvinism
Should I not pity Nineveh?
Jonah 4:11

Defining Hypercalvinism can be difficult at times, especially since there are so many variations of this doctrinal error. But I believe that the core failure of this system of thought centers in the question of the distribution of the Gospel message. For the Hypercalvinist, he believes that he is free from the obligations of the great commission through his faulty understanding of God's sovereign character. The line of reasoning is this: "God is sovereign, therefore we need not witness to others." This is the same form of *passive fatalism* that declares "Why does He still find fault? For who resists His will?" The logic behind such speculations is based

---

[171] Ephesians 2:4.
[172] See the Appendix for a more detailed presentation of this verse.

upon the same error of human reason. For the Hypercalvinist (whose doctrine has nothing to do with John Calvin, or the doctrines of grace), his faulty reasoning has led him to conclude that he can forsake evangelism, or even determine who should hear the Gospel message at all. Of the many errors that might be assigned to Hypercalvinism, this faulty concept of the Gospel mission is the greatest one of them all, and it is this same error that was at the root of Jonah's rebellion against the Lord. Jonah was not free to forsake the mission that was given to him, but despite this fact he tried to do so anyway. As you'll recall, Jonah was commanded by God to go to Nineveh and preach the Word of the Lord, but instead he rebelled and fled to Tarshish! After being swallowed and regurgitated by a large fish, Jonah reluctantly fulfilled his preaching duties in Nineveh. When the people repented, and the Lord withheld His wrath, Jonah became angry at the outcome and confessed to the Lord:

> *Jonah 4:2 And he prayed to the Lord and said, "Please Lord, was not this what I said while I was still in my own country? Therefore, in order to forestall this I fled to Tarshish, for I knew that Thou art a gracious and compassionate God, slow to anger and abundant in lovingkindness, and one who relents concerning calamity."*

God is gracious, abounding in lovingkindness, and He has ordained that men from every tribe, tongue, people, and nation will be saved throughout the earth. This great reality of God's abounding grace and mercy was the very truth that Jonah suppressed in unrighteousness, and thus he tried to flee from God's presence. Unfortunately, the spiritual progeny of Jonah's rebellion continues to this day. The tradition of Jonah is rooted in the false belief that the messenger has any authority over the Gospel message and its distribution. This tradition is also a conviction based upon denial: the denial of the Lord's broad love for all men *without distinction*. It is a denial of the fact that God's messengers are the instrumental means of the outworking of God's sovereign redemption; for how will they hear *without a preacher?*[173] And it is a denial of the fact that the Gospel of God is truly a universal message that is to be preached to all flesh – period! While the dark legacy of hypercalvinism is fairly recent, its primitive roots are indeed ancient. Throughout the generations, many have believed themselves to be the regulators of redemption, while often denying God's compassionate love for all mankind. The particular forms of these convictions will vary; however their doubly dead roots are all the same. Many today go about branding themselves as "Calvinists" who, by their own lives and doctrine, apparently know very little about John Calvin; most importantly, they know too little about the realities of the Scriptures themselves. God's Gospel is *gracious* and is to be extended to all men without any hesitancy or manipulation. Only Christ was able to declare omnisciently to the lost: "you will die in your sin; where I am going, you cannot come"[174] and to His disciples He said "did I Myself not choose you, the twelve, and yet one of you is a devil?"[175] But for the disciples of Christ, our knowledge is desperately limited; thus, the number of the elect and their identity cannot be *foreknown by men*. Even within the realm of professing Christendom, our ability to know (with certainty) those who are Christ's is yet imperfect.[176] For this reason, we must pray that the Word of God would *run* indiscriminately throughout the whole world, and that many would believe in the glorious Lamb of God![177]

---

[173] Romans 10:14.
[174] John 8:21.
[175] John 6:70.
[176] Matthew 13:24-30.
[177] 2 Thess. 3:1 As to the rest, pray ye, brethren, concerning us, that the word of the Lord may run and may be glorified... [YLT].

The Tradition of Unexceptional Love
*God loves you and has a wonderful
plan for your life*

Over the last half century, many Gospel tracts in America have undergone a dramatic change. Many of them presuppose things that are clearly off of the biblical mark by *minimizing the reality of man's sin,* while at the same time overemphasizing God's universal and beneficent love. A good number of these modern tracts begin with invitations such as: "How to have a happy and meaningful life" or as in the above case "God loves you and has a wonderful plan for your life." With such an approach, man's sinfulness is nominalized, as in this example: "According to the Bible sin is: *Failure to be what God wants us to be; *Failure to do what God wants us to do."[178] While these statements present some genteel truths regarding sin, they simply don't say enough in order to warn the hearer properly. For example, I could tell someone that a heart attack is just an event where someone has pain in the chest. While this indeed is true, it does not say enough about the extent of the pain, nor of the depth of danger which accompanies such a serious event! Gross understatements like these ultimately whitewash the reality of our sin and corruption, thereby minimizing the truth regarding mankind's present enmity with God and need for the Savior.[179] As a result, this will ultimately nominalize the Lord's pending wrath upon unrepentant sinners![180] Such an attempt to present the Gospel in a more favorable light actually results in the dimming of Christ's glorious love. Early in my Christian life, I remember reading a text

---

[178] Dallas Theological Seminary, How to have a happy and meaningful life (Dallas TX).
[179] Romans 5:10.
[180] John 3:36.

out of Revelation 14 that surprised me in light of the strength of the language:

> *Revelation 14:6-7: 6 And I saw another angel fly in the midst of heaven, having the everlasting gospel to preach unto them that dwell on the earth, and to every nation, and kindred, and tongue, and people, 7 Saying with a loud voice, Fear God, and give glory to him; for the hour of his judgment is come: and worship him that made heaven, and earth, and the sea, and the fountains of waters.*

When studying this important text, I couldn't help but to think to myself whether the people of our present generation would recognize the expressions "*fear God, give Him glory and worship Him*" as being a part of the message of the eternal Gospel![181] I just hope that in that day no one will attempt to correct that heavenly messenger by saying: "excuse me, but it goes like this: 'God loves you and has a wonderful plan for your life!'" This eternal Gospel message is a corrective to the contemporary message of today, in that it presents the Lord *as being the one who is worthy in the Gospel interaction*. Therefore, *He* is worthy to receive our reverence, our faith-filled declaration of His glory, and our devotion of worship. Instead of man's worthiness being the message, God's worthiness is the centerpiece of the Gospel. But messages which nominalize man's sin, and God's holy wrath against sin, end up with a confounding offer that I refer to as *upgrading*. This message of *upgrading* could be likened to moving from a small apartment to a larger condominium; that is, life is presently O.K., however you could receive the upgrade and have a more abundant life etc. In

---

[181] Having mentioned this verse, let me offer a side note. Concerning the many discussions that revolve around the question of the intent of God and evangelism, it should be noted that Revelation 14:6-7 reminds us that the Lord has always had the power and ability to bring about the complete evangelization of the world, and that, by just one angel.

terms of the fast-food market this would be called *supersizing*. In this paradigm, mankind is presented as being the worthy recipient of salvation such that the focus remains on what benefits he will receive through the Gospel transaction, to the exclusion of all other truths. But the Gospel is not about upgrading or supersizing. Men are in great danger. Because of their sin, they are at enmity with God and face the pending condemnation of His wrath and eternal judgment. The wrath of God abides on men, and will not be lifted until they bow the knee *in reverence* towards Him, confessing the *glory* of Christ in His sufficient work on the cross and through faith, entrusting themselves to the Savior as an act of *worship* before Him. And for those who do believe, they will escape the wrath of God[182] and be enveloped in His *exceptional love*, as the Father has for His own Son.[183] There is a profound difference between the messages of the Eternal Gospel and the passing "gospel" of our day.

THE TRADITION OF "WHOSOEVER" (WHOEVER CAME UP WITH WHOSOEVER?)

"Whosoever," surely meaneth me, Surely meaneth me,
O surely meaneth me;
J. Edwin McConnell[184]

The word *whosoever* has become an American theological construct in its own right. In some cases, entire songs, sermons, Gospel tracts, and books have relied heavily on this word in order to present a particular theological position. So is there a problem with the word *whosoever*? Not *per se*. The word whosoever is not

---

[182] Ephesians 2:3.

[183] John 15:9 As the Father hath loved me, so have I loved you: continue ye in my love.

[184] J. Edwin McConnell, Whosoever Surely Meaneth Me Eckert, P. (1998). *Steve Green's MIDI hymnal : A complete toolkit for personal devotions and corporate worship.* Oak Harbor, WA: Logos Research Systems, Inc.

intrinsically problematic, however, it is possible for one to use this word in either a right or wrong sense. Biblically speaking, this word is often used with respect to the general call of the Gospel, whether expressed by God or men. As to the latter case, the church is clearly called to proclaim the Gospel to all nations *indiscriminately*,[185] with the full confidence that those who are Christ's will eventually hear His voice and follow Him.[186] Therefore, the believer's *target audience* is an *indiscriminate* one such that the Gospel is offered to *whosoever will hear*. This is a reasonable and meaningful use of the word *whosoever* for the messengers of the church. It recognizes that, from man's perspective, we do not know, and cannot know, *who will come to Christ*. When speaking of this Gospel call, this word best represents the horizontal perspective of the human messenger such that there is something *uncertain* or *indefinite*[187] about who will be saved through the Gospel message. Assigning this sense of *uncertainty*, or *contingency*, to man's knowledge is entirely appropriate since, from man's point of view, the future is *uncertain* and *dependent upon many contingencies*. However, when we assign such *thoughts* to the Lord, we have a very serious problem because *nothing is uncertain or contingent to the omniscient and omnipotent God of the universe.*[188] Therefore, the

---

[185] Matthew 28:18-20.

[186] John 10:226-27.

[187] The Oxford English Dictionary identifies *whosoever* and *whoever* as having the same meaning. Both pronouns are used in a "generalized or indefinite sense" to communicate a measure of uncertainty. In some cases it can represent the same sense of uncertainty that is present in a conditional statement such as: "if any one." The Oxford English Dictionary 2nd Edition (Oxford University Press), Electronic Edition.

[188] Psalm 139:1-4 1 For the choir director. A Psalm of David. O Lord, Thou hast searched me and known me. 2 Thou dost know when I sit down and when I rise up; Thou dost understand my thought from afar. 3 Thou dost scrutinize my path and my lying down, And art intimately acquainted with all my ways. 4 Even before there is a word on my tongue, Behold, O Lord, Thou dost know it all.

word *whosoever* can be *misused* when thoughts of *mutability are assigned to the Lord Himself.* In fact, one can commit this error with any number of words. For example, the word *work* can be assigned to God[189] and man; however, the works of the Lord cannot be compared to any other since they are *immutably great, marvelous, righteous, and true.*[190] As well, the word holy can be used of to describe the angels[191] as well as the Lord Himself;[192] however, the Lord's holiness is, by quality, transcendent, such that He is *eternally holy* in all His perfections.[193] We can even say that men, by nature, possess a will that was originally created in the image and likeness of God; however, God's will is unique, being immutable, such that He is the only One who has the power and the authority to accomplish all that He as ordained. It should be obvious that any word that can be used to describe the Lord's *will*, His *works,* or His *nature,* can have a corrupting effect *if we impose the concepts of human sin or frailty on any one of them.* And so it is with the word *whosoever.* Therefore, when the word *whosoever* is used with respect to the Lord's cohortative and universal calls to mankind[194] such expressions represent a *general call to all men*, but they could never be interpreted as representing some uncertainty with God concerning His elect, or some contingency that might alter His eternal decree![195] The Lord knows who are His, by His sovereign will, as established from before the foundation of the

---

[189] John 5:17.
[190] Revelation 15:3-4.
[191] Daniel 4:23.
[192] Revelation 4:8.
[193] Revelation 16:5.
[194] The jussive and cohortative verbs often "express a command, or a wish." Psalm 81:8 "Hear, O My people, and I will admonish you; O Israel, if you would listen to Me!" Gesenius, F. W. (2003). Gesenius' Hebrew grammar (E. Kautzsch & S. A. E. Cowley, Ed.) (2d English ed.) (Page 321).
[195] Owen, The Death of Death, p. 329.

world;[196] therefore His general calls to mankind never represent any uncertainty or contingency to Him.

There Are Foolish Men On Both Sides Of The Argument

Let the search for Thy salvation,
Be our glory evermore[197]
Harry Emerson Fosdick

Harry Emerson Fosdick's grandmother once told him that if he couldn't believe in the story of Jonah and the fish that swallowed him, then he might as well surrender all of his Bible and his religion.[198]

Harry should have listened to his grandmother!

Anyone who has read Fosdick's work "The Modern Use of the Bible" will know that his message was a completely deconstructed one. The pages of Holy Writ were completely shredded beneath his knife of man centered thinking. To him, biblical truth was a mere tradition that was invented by men who needed a religion of conjured stories and miracles. Fosdick is considered to be one of the earliest pioneers of modern liberalism; a title that he clearly merited. Because his legacy of teaching is not always understood in the modern era, he is *sometimes* embraced as a model for Christian ministry in the present day. At the root of his error was the exaltation of man centered thinking – in its worst form. Even the man centeredness of his hymn "God of Grace and God of Glory" is clearly revealed in those words "Let the search for thy salvation, be

---

[196] 2 Timothy 2:19.
[197] Harry E. Fosdick, God of Grace and God of Glory, 1930.
[198] Harry Emerson Fosdick, The Living of These Days (Harper & Brothers, New York), p. 51.

our glory evermore." That's quite an admission: man's *search* for salvation is *his* glory evermore! This should serve as a reminder to us all that church history is filled with many theological potholes and detours. Because of this, one must be careful when journeying through it so as to avoid any serious collisions.

There appears to be an upsurge of interest in the subject of church history these days. Much of this can be profitable if one studies the subject beneath the authority of the Scriptures. But there is also an upsurge in *wrangling over church history*, such that many try to resolve the truths of Scripture through a debate over the theologians of the past. The problem with this approach is that, while the theologians of church history may be used as a *secondary witness to truth*, they can never be used as a *primary witness – that is the duty of Scripture alone*. No matter what hero one may choose from the past, it must be remembered that all were fallible men who possessed convictions that often grew and changed over the span of their lives. This does not mean that church history is irrelevant; not at all! These secondary witnesses from the past give us a source of needed accountability. Without them, we could be guilty of becoming doctrinal mavericks in the present day! But the rising controversy over the doctrine of the atonement is too often found in the wrong battlefield; the battlefield of history. It often smacks of the Pharisaical tradition found in the ancient writings of the Mishnah, which is a running commentary of historic sayings about the law. Line after line, the Mishnah's teachings are repeatedly prefaced with declarations of rabbinical authority, i.e., "Rabbi _____ says." The great error of it all is that the Rabbis of ancient history were made to be the *primary witnesses of truth*, rather than the Word of God. Such pharisaical patterns should serve as a severe warning to us all; when you read a work that is grounded deeply in arguments over church history, rather than

Scripture, then *beware*! The legacy of this approach to truth is a dangerous one. Of course on the other end of the spectrum, when people decide that they don't want to discuss the doctrines of Scripture at all, similar tactics are often employed. You have heard the expression: "Well, there are godly men on both sides of the discussion." This is a different use of church history. It is one that seeks to avoid a debate, rather than settle it. In contests such as these, the question often remains: "Are there *godly men* on both sides of any argument?" It could be, but such a statement settles nothing concerning the Word of God. In this line of thinking, all debates are thought to be settled by one's own assessment of the piety of past theologians; therefore, those who refuse to debate a particular matter will often find people on both sides of the contested doctrine whom they have deemed to be godly by their own estimation. Like a matter/anti-matter reaction, the substance of debate is thought to be annihilated simply by the interaction of past theologians. While this concept has validity in the realm of Physics, it offers no serious help to theologians who rest on the principle of *sola Scriptura*.

To be sure, church history has its important place: *beneath the authority of Scripture*. Should you ever be tempted to reverse that order, then just remember the frequent warnings given by our Savior concerning the deadly traditions of men. As with any doctrinal debate, the search for truth concerning Christ's atonement must be sought in the Scriptures alone!

ALL NATIONS UNDER GOD

CELEBRATING HIS VICTORY

FOR ALL ETERNITY

Fixing Our Eyes On Jesus

*Fixing our eyes on Jesus,
the author and perfecter of faith*
Hebrews 12:2

In an article published in December of 2002 by Popular Mechanics, entitled *The Real Face of Jesus*, a group of scientists claimed that they had formulated a method of recreating the face of Jesus using modern technologies and forensic anthropology. What was so interesting to me about it all was that the researchers spoke with such confidence that they had discovered what Jesus looked like, despite one little scientific shortcoming: "There is the additional problem of having neither a skeleton nor other bodily remains to probe for DNA."

Yes, that's because ... HIS BODY *ISN'T HERE ANYMORE!*

What exactly would we do without the scientific community? With powerful revelations such as these, even the most vulnerable among us are reminded that any "science" should be approached with a good measure of care and skepticism. But beyond the silliness of such a story, I do find it fascinating that the Scriptures offer us no details concerning Christ's physical features. I believe that it is a grace of God to us all that we don't know such things, for if we did men would begin fashioning the idols right away. If He had black, brown, ruddy, or pail hair then human prejudice would no longer care about skin color alone. His height, size, appearance, eye color would potentially become points of fixation that would distract many away from genuine worship. But spending time, money, and energy in an attempt to seek out that which God has not revealed is a complete waste of time. If the Lord wanted us to know what the incarnate Christ looked like, then we would have had that description given to us. A useless pursuit like this one should remind us all that the search for biblical truth can sometimes have very little to do with the Bible itself. Sometimes the church is like those presumptuous scientists – searching for a vision of Christ that is founded mostly upon human speculation, rather than on biblical reality. This is no harmless hobby; it is spiritually dangerous. The pale light of human reason is no match for the glory of God's Word. It is only by the vision of the victorious Lamb, who was standing *as if slain*, that the church is to be restored:

> *"Jesus wears the appearance of a slain Lamb as his court dress in which he wooed our souls, and redeemed them by his complete atonement. Nor are these only the ornaments of Christ: they are the trophies of his love and of his victory. He has divided the spoil with the strong. He has redeemed for himself a great multitude whom no man can number, and these scars are the memorials of the fight. Ah! if Christ thus loves to retain the thought of his sufferings for his people, how precious should his wounds be to us!"*

> *"Behold how every wound of his*
> *A precious balm distils,*
> *Which heals the scars that sin had made,*
> *And cures all mortal ills.*

> *Those wounds are mouths that preach his grace;*
> *The ensigns of his love;*
> *The seals of our expected bliss*
> *In paradise above."*[199]

May the church of God flee from *the despair of doubt* by *fixing her eyes upon Jesus* – the great Victor of our salvation. May Christ's bride forsake any doctrine which masquerades as a genuine

---

[199] Spurgeon, C. H. (1995). Morning and evening : Daily readings (April 23 PM). Oak Harbor, WA: Logos Research Systems, Inc.

testimony of His work, but which upholds an implicit message of failure. Faulty doctrines such as these, which are fashioned after the art and thought of man, will only send the church into a collision course with error and great sorrow. The end result can become a joyless assembly that has lost its way of following the Conqueror, *wherever He leads.*

HIS HOLY AND ETERNAL VICTORY
And I saw between the throne (with the four living creatures) and the elders a Lamb standing, as if slain...
Revelation 5:6

The body of Christ has the great privilege of fixing her eyes upon the true and biblical vision of Christ. As mentioned before, there are no biblical descriptions of Christ's physical appearance when He walked this earth, however, the Scriptures do provide us with one, beautiful description of the *glorified* Christ - *from His hair down to His feet*:

> *Revelation 1:12-17: 12 Then I turned to see the voice that spoke with me. And having turned I saw seven golden lampstands, 13 and in the midst of the seven lampstands One like the Son of Man, clothed with a garment down to the feet and girded about the chest with a golden band. 14 His head and hair were white like wool, as white as snow, and His eyes like a flame of fire; 15 His feet were like fine brass, as if refined in a furnace, and His voice as the sound of many waters; 16 He had in His right hand seven stars, out of His mouth went a sharp two-edged sword, and His countenance was like the sun shining in its strength. 17 And when I saw Him, I fell at His feet as dead. But He laid His right hand on me, saying to me, "Do not be afraid; I am the First and the Last.*

Not a single resident of this planet can claim a resemblance to all that John saw in this vision. What the Apostle saw was so compelling and transcendent that he fell to the ground as a dead man! This penetrating vision is one which conveys the purity, holiness, power, omniscience, and judgment of Christ. It also reminds us that as the Lamb of God, He was *unblemished* and *without sin* in every way.[200] This is why John gives us that description of Christ in Revelation chapter 5:

> *Revelation 5:6 And I saw between the throne (with the four living creatures) and the elders a Lamb standing, as if slain...*

What does it mean to see something that is standing *as if it had been slain?* The surreal nature of this vision may not strike the casual reader at first, but understand that this word *slain* [*esphagmenon*] is frequently used to speak of animal sacrifices, and it is even used to speak of the Messiah's sacrifice in Isaiah 53:7.[201] The point is simply this: slain animals are not in the habit of standing, or doing anything for that matter. What John saw was not some puzzle designed to challenge his intellect, rather it was a remarkably beautiful picture of the Lamb's victorious death (slain) and resurrection life (standing). Though He was dead, now He is alive. But would this have been true if there were any blemish or failure in this Lamb? Had there been any stain of sin or deception, then there would have been no victory over sin and death. You see, the victory of Christ's atonement was a victory of absolute holiness. Without His purity, perfection, and righteousness His blood would not be *unblemished* and therefore we would remain dead in our trespasses and sins. But our Savior is infinitely holy and pure, for He cannot sin, nor does He ever lie. What He promised to do for His own, whom He loved to the end, [202]will be done in eternal glory:

---

[200] Christ is called the Lamb of God 31 times in the book of Revelation.
[201] Isaiah 53:7 7 He was oppressed and He was afflicted, Yet He opened not His mouth; He was led as a lamb to the slaughter, And as a sheep before its shearers is silent, So He opened not His mouth.
[202] John 13:1.

John 10:28-29: 28 and I give eternal life to them, and they shall never perish; and no one shall snatch them out of My hand. 29 My Father, who has given them to Me, is greater than all; and no one is able to snatch them out of the Father's hand.

Revelation 21:4 and He shall wipe away every tear from their eyes; and there shall no longer be any death; there shall no longer be any mourning, or crying, or pain; the first things have passed away.

Both of these texts supply the believer with a treasury of truth and hope. Particularly, Revelation 21:4 stands as the surety of our eternal life in Heaven, for literally speaking, "the death *will not be.*" The future indicative verb (*will not be*) in that statement establishes the sure, immutable fact that death will never again enter the sphere of our existence. Some time ago, a few of my children asked me a question about this important verse in Revelation 21:4. They wanted to know if there would be another fall, like that which happened with Adam in the garden. They surmised that since Adam was created in holiness, perhaps there could be the possibility of a repeat of sin in future glory. Without a moment of hesitation, I quickly responded with an answer of - *no.* The plain and simple truth is that God, *whose oaths and promises are sure* (because He cannot lie), will never allow the risen saints to fall into the error of Adam. You see, *the death will not be.* Thanks be to God that we will not be free to commit sin! The eternal praise and glory of God rests upon this promise, and I can confidently say to you *that He will be glorified.*[203] Once again, we find that our hope of eternal redemption rests upon the *immutable power and promises of our Lord*:

---

[203] John 12:28 "Father, glorify Thy name." There came therefore a voice out of heaven: "I have both glorified it, and will glorify it again."

> Intent(Eternal Life – John 10:28-29) ≫ Effect(Eternal Life – Rev. 21:4) = **Eternal Victory**

The church of Jesus Christ needs desperately to fall as a dead man at the sight of the unblemished Lamb who, though slain, now stands forevermore. This glorious, sinless, and eternal Lamb of God is the very centerpiece of human history, and will be the centerpiece of our eternal worship and praise. His unblemished life, work, and promises supply us with an eternal foundation in glory that will never falter or fail.

ADORING THE LAMB OF GOD FOREVER
And the four living creatures kept saying, "Amen." And the elders fell down and worshiped.
Revelation 5:14

One thing that I love about these precious worship scenes, found in the book of Revelation, is the fact we can be certain that they are acts of *perfect worship.* By contrast, a perusal of the New Testament reveals some very imperfect worship taking place in many of the churches of that day; but in glory – it's all perfect! Holy angels and glorified saints joined together, without the veil of sin, are seen in these explosive moments of loving adoration and loud praise. I am convinced that the modern church has traded in such essential lessons of worship, for an eschatological time-table instead. In a similar vein, the doctrine of the atonement has often been reduced to a battle of plastic robots, rather than being reverently embraced as the very centerpiece of our worship, adoration, and practice in this life, and in the life to come. But by God's grace, the church can; no, it *must break away* from this prison of contemporary pettiness. The contemplation of Christ's sacrifice, and His shed blood for our sins, provides us with a sure foundation of hope and joyful ministry which looks to Christ alone as our Victor:

> *Matthew 26:26-30: And as they were eating, Jesus took bread, blessed and broke it, and gave it to the disciples and said, "Take, eat; this is My body." 27 Then He took the cup, and gave thanks, and gave it to them, saying, "Drink from it, all of you. 28 "For this is My blood of the new covenant, which is shed for many for the remission of sins. 29 "But I say to you, I will not drink of this fruit of the vine from now on until that day when I drink it new with you in My Father's kingdom." 30 And when they had sung a hymn, they went out to the Mount of Olives.*

O how the saints of God do long to attend the heavenly wedding feast which is now previewed in the blessed table of our Lord. With each and every act of participation in the Lord's Table, we remember *Him in His death*, and *in His victory*. In the meantime, He patiently waits to partake of the cup of His covenant in glory with us; in that day He will return for His bride to take her home forever. Here is our affectionate remembrance and anticipation of our glorious bridegroom, the Lamb of God, as expressed in this hymn which is based upon the writings of Samuel Rutherford:

> *1. The sands of time are sinking, the dawn of heaven breaks;*
> *The summer morn I've sighed for, the fair, sweet morn awakes;*
> *Dark, dark hath been the midnight, but dayspring is at hand;*
> *And glory, glory dwelleth in Immanuel's land.*
>
> *2. The King there in His beauty without a veil is seen;*
> *It were a well-spent journey, though sev'n deaths lay between;*
> *The Lamb with His fair army, doth on Mount Zion stand;*
> *And glory, glory dwelleth in Emmanuel's land.*
>
> *3. O Christ, He is the fountain, the deep sweet well of love;*
> *The streams of earth I've tasted, more deep I'll drink above;*

> There to an ocean fullness, His mercy doth expand;
> And glory, glory dwelleth in Emmanuel's land.

> 4. The bride eyes not her garment, but her dear bridegroom's face;
> I will not gaze at glory, but on my King of grace;
> Not at the crown He gifteth, but on His pierced hand;
> The Lamb is all the glory, of Emmanuel's land.[204]

Indeed, *the Lamb is all the glory, of Emmanuel's land!* On that glorious day, we will sing *a new song,* the *song of the Lamb,* and thus declare His praise for all time. The veil will be lifted forevermore and we will behold our glorious Bridegroom in all His splendor. The saints of God will dwell there in glory as a precious expression of the Son's eternal and infallible love for the Father – a love in which Christ's bride will be enveloped for days without end. In that day no one will cry out "why have you made me thus?" No one will bemoan the absence of Adam's *freedom to fall in sin.* No one will wonder why the Lord did not dispatch His myriads of myriads, and thousands of thousands of angels into the earth *to* preach the eternal Gospel to its every inhabitant - *in every generation.*[205] In that day, no one will complain that the number of saints in heaven are too few; instead, the children of God will all marvel that the Lord was graciously willing *to save any at all*; and our sense of wonder will be overwhelmed by the sight of, not a few, but a countless number of the redeemed, whom the Lord saved for His own glory and good pleasure. Ultimately, our affection and worship will have this centerpiece in glory: *the victorious Lamb of God who suffered and died for our sins.* Until that precious day comes, may the

---

[204] The Sands of Time are Sinking: based upon the letters of Samuel Rutherford and written by Anne R. Cousin, (Trinity Hymnal, Great Commission Publications, Suwanee GA, 1995), p. 546.
[205] Revelation 14:6-7.

church melt in loving humility and joyful contrition in the presence of her great Champion and Victor: the Lord Jesus Christ.

Our precious Lord Jesus, come quickly!

All Nations Under God

Appendix:

Rightly Dividing The Word

Rightly Dividing the Word

Be diligent to present yourself approved to God,
a worker who does not need to be ashamed,
rightly dividing the word of truth.
2 Timothy 2:15

Benjamin Franklin was often bothered by religious people who sought to argue for the Bible's veracity, but who also failed to possess any significant knowledge of the very book they tried to defend. Because of this, he loved to debate Bible doctrine with others such that he had the habit of testing his opponents' knowledge in a unique way. After a round of unresolved debate he would often say: "Give me a day to think the matter over, for [I know that] I'm correct." Immediately, he would go to his print shop and set up his printing press with some print type that was typically used for Bibles. Modifying a biblical text with his own thoughts and anecdotes, he printed his position and argument in biblical sounding language. He would then return the next day to his opponents and proudly present them with the proof of his argument to see if his religious victims would concede to him or discern his trickery.[206]

Therefore, we can thank Mr. Franklin for that historic and extra-biblical saying: *"God helps those who help themselves."*

For Mr. Franklin, it was all a joke. Sadly, for many in today's church, *this is how they "do" theology.* But the Word of God should never be used as a means of trickery, or as a flexible instrument to be used in

---

[206] Poor Richard's Almanac (or sometimes "Richard Saunders") ran from 1732 – 1757 and was published by Benjamin Franklin. It offered practical suggestions, recipes, advice on personal hygiene, and folksy urgings to be frugal, industrious, and orderly. It is here that he popularized those well known sayings: "God helps those who help themselves."

one's personal battles. The *sword of the Spirit*, is the propriety of God alone, and it must be treated as such - *without compromise*. But it seems that there are some passages which frequently fall prey to the atonement debate, whether they should or not. In the worst of cases, many of these texts are merely glossed over with very little exegetical care, and are then used as a kind of mantra in someone's theological rant. But such tactics must be avoided! The serious student of Scripture must always ask crucial questions of any text before ever using that text in a broader theological system of thought. Such a careful study requires a reverence for the Lord and His Word (Isaiah 66:2); a conviction of the absolute inspiration and infallibility of all Holy Writ (Matthew 5:18); and it requires the understanding that no Scripture is to be subject to a man's own private interpretations (2 Peter 1:20-21). Such warnings and reminders are important, for even the best of men in life will struggle with the battle of objective interpretation; however it is a necessary battle which requires hard work and a serious mind. Therefore, in the following pages I will be presenting several passages, some of which have fallen prey to some measure of misuse in the atonement war. These texts will be presented *diagrammatically*, so that the reader can graphically see the argument of each text.

CHRIST'S VICTORIOUS ATONEMENT
Worthy is the Lamb who was slain
Revelation 5:9

As we saw in Revelation chapter 5, John wept because he momentarily thought that no one was *worthy* to take the scroll and to break its seals. His grief was gloriously shattered by the vision of the glorious Son of God when He appeared as a lamb, standing as if slain. Christ's worthiness was established by the fact that He was the One who was victorious [*enikēsen*] through His sacrifice on the cross. The main premise of the Song of the Lamb is therefore found in the description of His *worthiness* [*axios*] in view of His *sacrifice* and *purchase for God:*

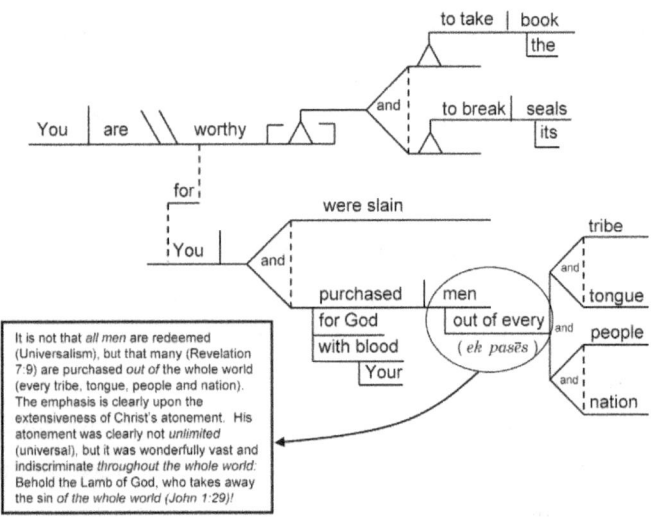

As is made clear by the above graph, the bounty of Christ's redemption is described in terms of a great number already purchased throughout the whole world – *ek pasēs: out of every tribe and tongue and people and nation*. The partitive expression *ek pasēs* clearly rules out the possibility of universalism, but heralds an *extensive atonement* in light of its worldwide effect. Such a view of the extensive nature of Christ's work underscores the principle of the Great Commission.[207] It also reminds us of the indicative nature of God's decree and His redemptive work:

> "...if the proffer be (as they say) universal, and the intention of God be answerable thereunto,-that is, He intends the salvation of them to whom the tender of it upon faith is made, or may be so; then,-*First*, What becomes of election and reprobation? Nether of them, certainly, can consist with this universal purpose of saving us all. *Secondly*, If He

---

[207] Owen, The Death of Death, p. 299.

intend it, why is it, then, not accomplished? Doth He fail of His purpose?"[208]

The song of the Lamb is not a dirge or lament of failure. Such a song of rejoicing *and victory* helps to calibrate our thinking, not only about the *extent of the Gospel mission* in this world, but especially about the *infallibility of the Lord's promises* in everything!

HIS UNIVERSAL *AND* EXCEPTIONAL LOVE
For God so loved the world...
John 3:16 [YLT]

There are many verses over which great confusion has been generated because of the word whosoever; but for our purposes here we will look at the most popular one of them all – John 3:16:

> *John 3:16 For God so loved the world, that he gave his only begotten Son, that whosoever believeth on him should not perish, but have eternal life. [ASV]*

This precious, subordinate clause clearly shows us the divine purpose for which God gave His only begotten Son: *to save all believers.* Certainly, those who will come to faith are already foreordained by God, as we have already seen in Scripture. Theologically, the word whosoever doesn't present a conflict here, especially if one does not assign the corrupting thought of human uncertainty to Christ's expression. However, the word *whosoever* is really not the best choice based upon the Greek text, and the context overall. Consider this same verse in Young's Literal Translation:

---

[208] Ibid., 312.

John 3:16 for God did so love the world, that His Son— the only begotten — He gave, that <u>every one who is believing</u> in him may not perish, but may have life age-during.[209][YLT]

He gave His Son – *that every one who is believing* in Him may not perish. Young's literal translation conveys the appropriate construction of the Greek (*pas o pisteuōn*): literally, *all those believing*. This is why Young's Literal Translation uses the expression *everyone who believes* rather than *whosoever believes*. The more literal translation reveals that John 3:16 is particularly – *particular*. There is a *particular* group for whom the Son was given - *all who will believe*:

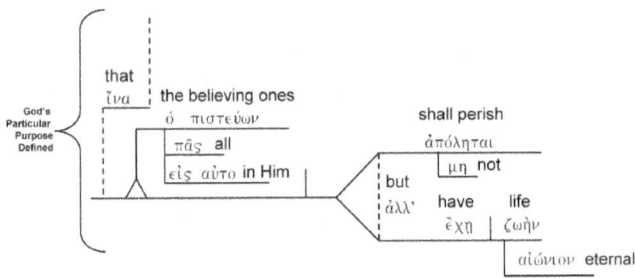

No matter what one does to John 3:16, it cannot be concluded that it represents some *uncertainty* or *contingency* to God! The fact that *we don't know who will believe* is another matter entirely.

I mentioned earlier that John 3:16 is a subordinate clause, and it is; it is subordinate to the thoughts previously developed in verses 14-15, where Christ teaches Nicodemus about His redemptive mission:

John 3:14-16: 14 'And as Moses did lift up the serpent in the wilderness, so it behoveth the Son of Man to be lifted up, 15 that every one who is

---

[209] Young, R. (1997). <u>Young's literal translation</u>. Oak Harbor: Logos Research Systems.

APPENDIX

believing in him may not perish, but may have life age-during, 16 for God did so love the world, that His Son—the only begotten—He gave, that every one who is believing in him may not perish, but may have life age-during. [YLT]

As Moses lifted up the serpent in the wilderness, so must the Son of Man be lifted up that *every one believing in Him* may not perish. As of verse 15, Nicodemus must have been filled with anticipation to hear about the eternal life that was to be offered through the Son of Man. Contextually speaking, Christ's mention of Moses and the brazen serpent would have refreshed Nicodemus' memory regarding God's kindness and severity in dealing with *the nation of Israel*. It is here that Christ offers an interesting comparison concerning His own mission to that of Moses, by using the word "as." The strength of this comparative particle *kathōs* (as) is often underestimated in the overall context of John 3. By using this word, Christ established a comparative contrast between Himself and Moses. What Moses offered to the *nation of Israel* was quite different to what the Savior would accomplish *throughout the whole world*. This contextual development of John 3:14-16 is very important, for in verse 14 God's gracious offer of deliverance was offered to the whole nation of Israel; but by contrast, in verses 15-16, His gracious love is manifested through His Gospel offer *to the whole world*; and while all believers *in the land of Israel* found *temporal deliverance* through God's provision of the brazen serpent (v. 14), we understand that all believers *throughout the world* will be delivered *eternally* through Christ's death on the cross (vs. 15-16). Thus,

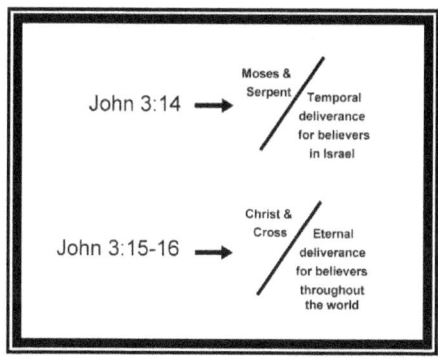

151

Christ's mention of Moses, by itself, would have drawn Nicodemus' thoughts to the limitations of national Israel (via of Numbers 21); but Christ did not leave him with such a limited thought. Instead, He *extended* His description of God's love to include *the whole world of sinners!*

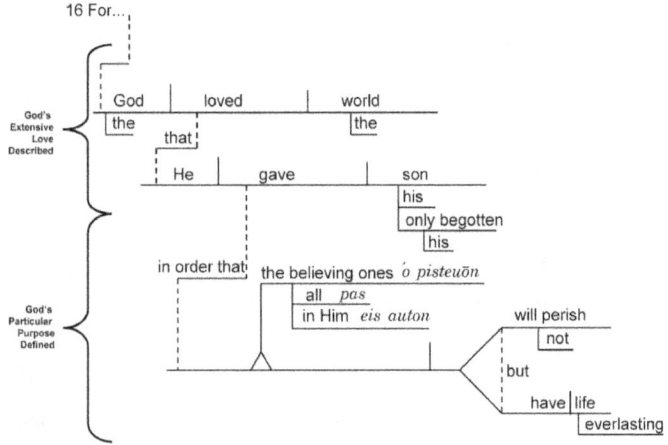

John 3:14-16: 14 "As Moses lifted up the serpent in the wilderness, even so must the Son of Man be lifted up;

15 so that whoever believes will in Him have eternal life.

This comparison between Moses and Christ thus magnifies God's *universal* and *exceptional* love. For example, the Lord was lovingly gracious and patient towards *all of Israel*, but only those who believed in Him were finally delivered from His wrath. Similarly, the Lord is lovingly gracious and patient towards the whole world, but only those who believe in Christ *will not perish, but have everlasting life*. The celebrated truth of John 3:16 heralds the reality of God's gracious love for the world of His creation, while upholding His exceptional devotion to those who pay homage to His only Son through faith in Him.[210]

---

[210] Psalm 2:12 Kiss the Son, lest He be angry, And you perish in the way, When His wrath is kindled but a little. Blessed are all those who put their trust in Him.

The Tradition of Cancelled Sin
He breaks the pow'r
of canceled sin...

One of the confounding questions that inherently comes with the doctrine of universal atonement, is that of sin's present power and dominion. The question that naturally arises is: "If Christ's sacrifice *actually atoned for* the sins of all men (universally), then what is the unbeliever's present state?" By arguing that the sins of all men have been atoned, the Universalist presents a confounding message concerning man's bondage in sin. The famous hymn, *O For A Thousand Tongues To Sing,* sustains this same confusion:

He breaks the pow'r of canceled sin,
He sets the pris'ner free;
His blood can make the foulest clean;
His blood availed for me.

One has to wonder: what power can *cancelled sin* have? While the rest of the verse seems to steer us in a better direction, our question still remains. It is at this point that the great dilemma of universal atonement enters into the very Gospel message itself. If the sins of men are *already cancelled* through the atonement of Christ, then what is the Gospel messenger to say about the unbeliever's *actual need*? Those who advocate that the debt of sin has been cancelled for all men (*without exception*) often do so based upon a faulty interpretation of Colossians 2:14-15. Paul's mention of the *cancellation of the debt of our sin,* which was *taken away when He nailed it to the cross,* is entirely subordinate to the primary clause: He made *you* alive. Therefore, such statements concerning the cancellation of debt are designed to clarify the details of God's work of salvation in the life of a *believer*:

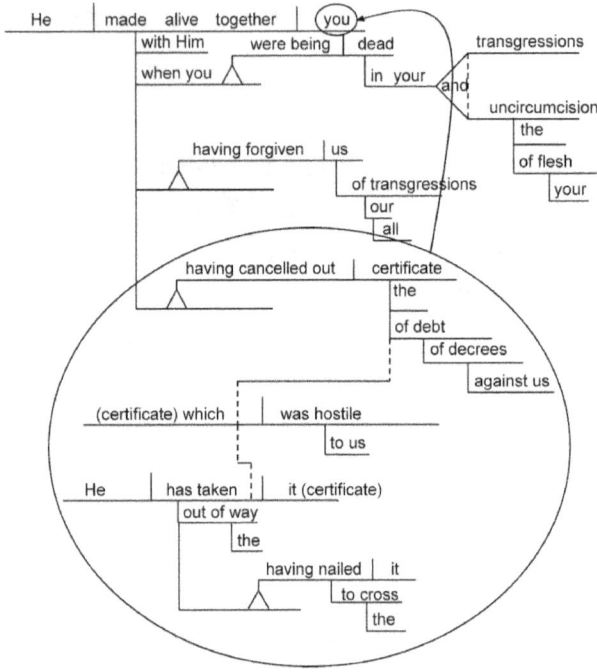

Obviously, the "you" in verse 13 can only refer to believers *who have been made alive.* For *them* the debt of sin has been cancelled, as is obvious from the *subordinate clauses circled above.* Beyond this clear description of the believer's salvation, there is no textual evidence that would lead one to argue that the certificate of debt has been cancelled for *all men without exception.* The fact that such a debt remains explains why it is that Christ calls the unbeliever a slave to sin:

> John 8:34-36: 34 Jesus answered them, "Most assuredly, I say to you, whoever commits sin is a slave of sin. 35 "And a slave does not abide in the house forever, but a son abides forever. 36 "Therefore if the Son makes you free, you shall be free indeed.

The faulty notion of a universal cancellation of sin's debt renders violence against the teachings of Christ Himself. *All men are slaves because of their sin*, and will remain so until the Son makes them free. Until they are freed through faith in Christ, they remain in bondage and are culpable for the debt of their own sin. The privilege of cancellation of such debt is the sole privilege of those who have life and genuine freedom in Christ alone.

God Is Patient Toward *You*
...regard the patience of our Lord as salvation.
2 Peter 3:15

Earlier in this book, we considered the important subject of God's universal love. We noted that the Lord's love is patient, kind, and full of compassion and that it was by His *lovingkindness* that He appeared to mankind, endowed with salvation[211] (Titus 3:4), offering the gracious Gospel to all men without distinction (Matthew 28:18-20). We also noted that it was by the Lord's *loving patience* that He has endured the many generations of sinful men (1 Peter 3:20)[212] such that He does not delight in the death of the wicked, but instead He graciously calls all to repentance (Ezekiel 18:23). These truths remind us of the Lord's great patience towards mankind. This latter theme is particularly strong in both of Peter's epistles where he offers an important look at the Lord's patience with the lost (2 Peter 3:3-7) exercised for the sake of His elect (1 Peter 3:20, 2 Peter 3:8-15). This concept of God's patience towards mankind is often misunderstood, particularly in 2 Peter chapter 3. 2 Peter 3:9 is often cited for the purpose of supporting the notion that God intends to save everyone *without exception*:

---

[211] Titus 3:4 But when the kindness and the love of God our Savior toward man appeared...

[212] 1 Peter 3:20 ...when the patience of God kept waiting in the days of Noah, during the construction of the ark, in which a few, that is, eight persons, were brought safely through the water.

> *2 Peter 3:9 The Lord is not slow about His promise, as some count slowness, but is patient toward you, not wishing for any to perish but for all to come to repentance.*

This wonderful text teaches us an important truth about the patience of God and His work of salvation. But what is often missed in this important text is the proper identity of the very recipients of God's patience. Peter declares that "God is patient towards you." But who is in view when he says *"you"*? Once again, the context of Peter's statement is crucial. In the beginning of 2 Peter chapter 3 Peter speaks of God's *patient endurance* with the "mockers" and "ungodly men" (vs. 3-7). He then transitions from his third person plural references to these ungodly men (vs. 3-7), to a different audience whom he addresses in the *second person plural*: those who are believers in Christ (vs. 8-15). In this latter portion of 2 Peter chapter 3, we have a description of God's particular purposes in exercising patience, which is *to bring to repentance all who are His beloved in Christ.*

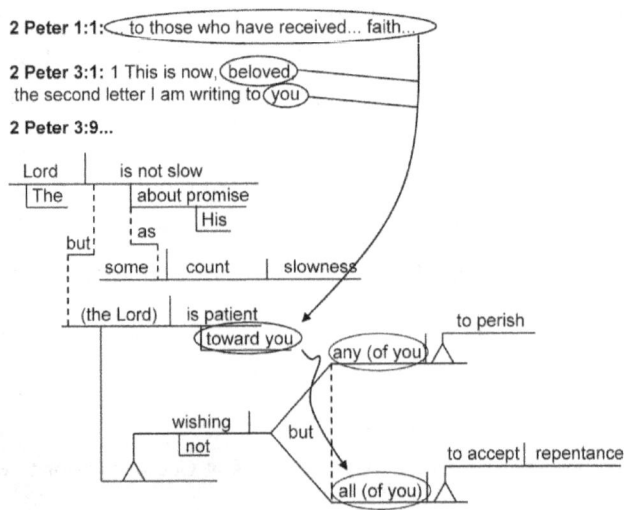

When Peter described the Lord's patience, he clearly stated that the Lord is patient toward *"you."* The context clearly reveals that Peter referred to God's beloved of his generation, and by inference, to God's children of every generation. This is the very same patience that the Lord showed for the sake of Noah and his family:

> *1 Peter 3:19-20: 19 ... He [Christ] went and made proclamation to the spirits now in prison, 20 who once were disobedient, when the patience of God kept waiting in the days of Noah, during the construction of the ark, in which a few, that is, eight persons, were brought safely through the water.*

Through His great patience, the Lord endured the wickedness of mankind for the sake of delivering only Noah and his family. This patient deliverance of Noah is a type of salvation,[213] reminding us all that the Lord exercises His patience towards *all men without exception*, so that none of His elect will perish, but all will come to repentance and genuine faith in Christ – *at the time of His sovereign choosing.*

No One Has The Power
I will raise him up on the last day
John 6:44

One verse that is often introduced within the discussion of the atoning work of Christ is John 6:44. While this text does not address the matter of the atonement by itself, it is often consulted in light of its statements concerning the effectual call of God's elect. This verse is only relevant to the degree that it helps us to see the relationship between God's general call, and His effectual call of His people. If universal atonement were true, then texts such as John

---

[213] 1 Peter 3:21.

6:44 raise serious questions about the very nature of God's call. Whereas Christ's description of the Father's work of drawing sinners is presented as being effectual, the advocate of universal atonement is instead stuck with the conclusion that God is many times *ineffectual* in His work of drawing sinners to Himself. In other words, God is trying, but man is powerfully resisting. Therefore, a great portion of universal atonement embraces this thought of God trying to save everyone, but that He hasn't the sufficient *power or willingness* to save everyone in light of their rebellion. Such a scheme of thought ends up exalting the power of man's will, while reducing the power of God to a cajoling whimper. But the Scriptures clearly teach that all men who are condemned are so because of their own sin, not because God was powerless to save them. Just how *powerful* or *powerless* is the human will? Can man come to Christ in faith of his own volition and strength? The clear answer from Scripture is – *no*. Most translations of John 6:44 use the word *can*, for the words of Christ: "no one *can come* to me unless the Father... draws him." The word *can* isn't problematic or wrong, it just happens to be flat. After all, *dunamis*, from which we get the English word *dynamite*, is far more compelling than the word *can*. And draw, *elkōn* [to drag] has a much stronger force in the original. Put together, John 6:44 has a very forceful message about the *strength of God* and the *powerlessness of man*:

John 6:44

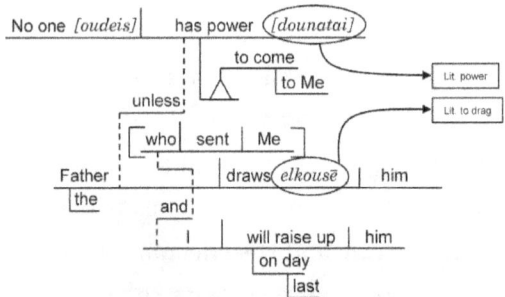

The clarity and simplicity of this passage is very important for it reveals man's *inability* to come to Christ apart from the power of God.²¹⁴ I often tell people that men are absolutely *powerless* to come to Christ. When asked for justification for my use of the word *powerless*, I immediately take them to this important text. The truth is that men are *powerless* to come to Christ *unless* the Father sovereignly draws them by *His power* and through *His Word* (John 6:45).

HE GAVE THEM THE RIGHT TO BECOME CHILDREN
who were born, not of blood nor of the will of the flesh
nor of the will of man, but of God.
John 1:13

Consider the following graph and note carefully the aorist verbs and the repeated identity of *those who believe*:

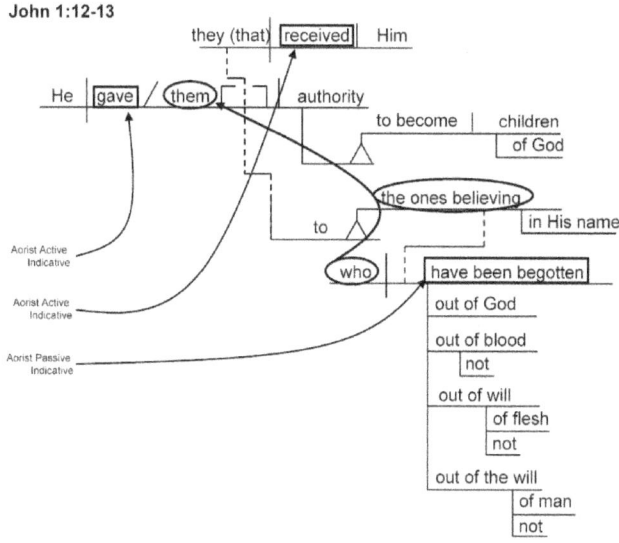

---

²¹⁴ The passive verb *dounatai* is followed by the complementary infinitive *elthein* [to come]. This infinitive serves as an adverb, completing the thought of the intransitive verb. For a more complete examination of the adverbial use of the infinitive, see: Wallace, Greek Grammar, pp. 590-599.

It is sometimes argued that John 1:12-13 shows that *it does depend on the man who wills*, after all, John says: *to those who received Him, to them He gave the right to become children of God!* But the fact that John begins, in verse 12, with the sinner's act of believing, does nothing to exalt the human will above God's work of grace. Instead, when one looks carefully at the full text of verses 12 *and* 13, it is observed that the ones who *actively* received Him were the same ones who were *passively begotten of God to begin with ("have been begotten")*. Verse 13 takes it all a step further when John tells us that these believers *were passively begotten* – not by blood, nor by flesh, nor of the will of man, but entirely *"out of"* God. The very source of the *active will* of the believer, mentioned in verse 12, is therefore clarified in verse 13. All three aorist verbs speak of completed action and therefore do not emphasize a temporal sequence; however the passivity of the expression *"have been begotten"* [*egennēthēsan*] shows us a logical order of thought. It explains to us that men are made alive, not by blood, or the will of the flesh, or the will of man, but *out of God*. Therefore, men believe (actively) because of God's work of begetting new life (*have been begotten*). This presentation of truth is quite characteristic of John, as we see repeatedly expressed in his first epistle:

- *1 John 2:29 ...every one doing the righteousness, of him hath been begotten. [YLT]*

- *1 John 4:7 ...every one who is loving, of God he hath been begotten. [YLT]*

- *1 John 5:1 Every one who is believing that Jesus is the Christ, of God he hath been begotten [YLT]*

This familiar construction in John's epistle reminds us of the important priority of new birth. These three statements are filled

APPENDIX

with the reminder of the Savior's teaching that *unless one is born again, he cannot see the kingdom of God.*[215] Thus, the Apostle's grammatical pattern repeats a very important truth concerning the *priority* of God's work of regeneration:

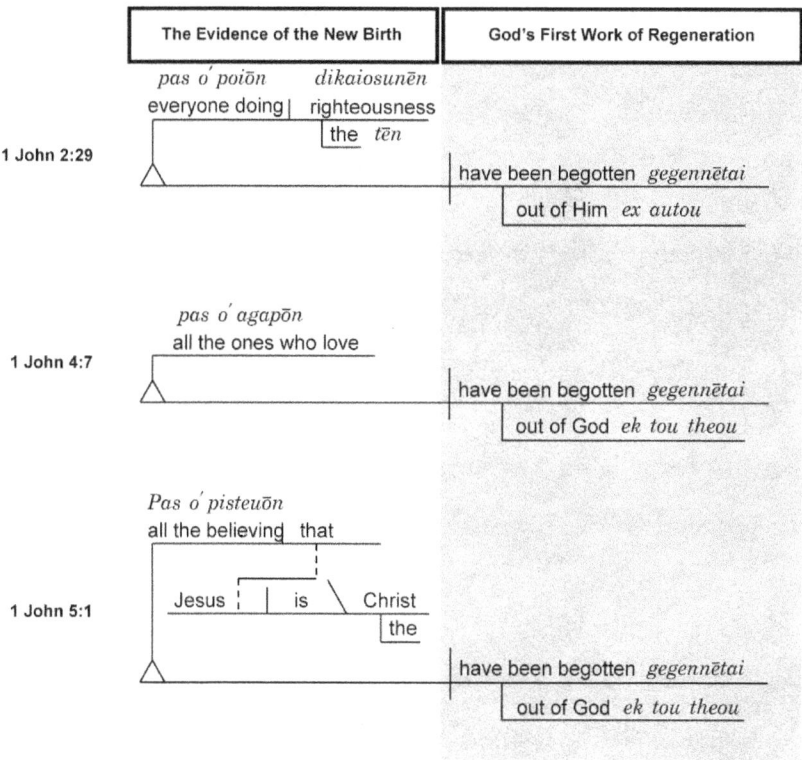

Those who *presently* practice righteousness, manifest godly love, and believe that Jesus is the Christ [*all present active participles*], do so because they *have been, antecedently, begotten of God* [*gegennētai* - Perfect passive indicative verb]. Therefore the fruit of the Spirit's work in the life of a believer[216] has one root found in

---

[215] John 3:3 Jesus answered and said to him, "Truly, truly, I say to you, unless one is born again, he cannot see the kingdom of God."

[216] Galatians 5:22-23: 22 And the fruit of the Spirit is: Love, joy, peace, long-suffering, kindness, goodness, faith, 23 meekness, temperance. [YLT].

God's initial act of imparting new life to those whom He chose before the foundation of the world,[217] that they should be drawn to saving faith and loving obedience[218] in Christ.[219]

John's point is clear, both in his first epistle and in his Gospel: men are not *born again* by virtue of their genealogy (not out of blood), nor *out of* the will of man's frail flesh (not *out of* the will of the flesh), nor *out of* the corrupt and impotent will of the inner man (nor *out of* the will of man) – but *out of God alone*. Therefore sonship, and faith itself, are gifts from God who alone gives life to those who are *spiritually dead* and *powerless* to come to Christ.

---

[217] John Murray, Redemption, Accomplished and Applied (WM. B. Eerdman's Publishing Company, Grand Rapids Michigan), pp. 103-104.

[218] Ephesians 2:10 For we are His workmanship, created in Christ Jesus for good works, which God prepared beforehand, that we should walk in them.

[219] Acts 13:48 And when the Gentiles heard this, they began rejoicing and glorifying the word of the Lord; and as many as had been appointed to eternal life believed.

Index

A

Apocalypse
    the book of Revelation, 20, 21, 22, 49, 86, 139, 141
    eschatology, 21, 22, 141
Atonement
    extent of, 31, 43, 45 - 46, 48, 53, 71, 75, 76, 79, 81, 86
    intent of, 28, 29, 43, 48
    effect of, 3, 7, 8, 23, 24, 25, 27, 29, 44, 45, 46, 51, 56, 89, 125

B

Biblical authority, 14–19
Bitterness, in the church, 13

C

Calling
    effectual, 70
Children of God, 25, 37, 48, 57, 65, 67, 81, 96, 107, 108, 159
    adoption, 33, 62, 65, 66, 67, 68, 123
Christ, 25, 31, 36, 42, 115
    His holiness, 36, 37, 139, 141
    His love for the Father, 34, 35, 36, 37, 43, 48, 96, 97
    His servanthood, 69
    His sheep, 24
    His priestly office, 70
    the Bridegroom of the church, 70
    the Father's love for, 46, 62
    the Good Shepherd, 69
    the High Priest, 70
    the Victor, 19, 42, 45, 46, 71, 85
    victorious atonement, 18, 19, 22, 24, 26, 28, 30, 31, 42, 53, 78, 92, 115
Church
    contemporary, 14, 39, 90
    contention in, 12–13, 14, 49, 53, 85
    despair in, 24, 26, 92, 112, 115
Clichés, doctrine established by, 16, 17, 19, 120
Creedalism, 120

D

Discipline, 66, 67, 68

E

Evangelism, 109, 112, 119, 128
Exceptional Love
    of a Heavenly citizen, 104
    of a husband, 15, 97, 98, 101, 105

of a wife, 70, 97, 99, 100, 101, 102, 105
of the brethren, 67, 106, 107, 112, 114, 126

F

Foreordination, 41, 60, 110, 149
Free will, 123

G

God
    His decrees, 20, 26, 29, 32, 33, 34, 38, 39, 40, 41, 42, 43, 46, 49, 61, 62, 68, 70, 71, 105, 113, 131, 140
    His authority, 14, 17
    His beneficence, 66
    His exceptional love, 53, 62, 66, 67, 68, 69, 70, 71, 101, 105, 106, 107, 108, 109, 129
    His good pleasure, 29, 31
    His grace, 55–56
    His immutability, 38, 39, 41, 43, 46, 62, 71, 77, 131, 140
    His mercy, 54–55
    His sovereign love, 57, 63
    His sovereign mercy, 57, 60, 61, 62, 71, 110, 114
    His sovereignty (general), 58, 63, 64, 110, 111, 112, 113, 114, 118, 119
    His transcendence, 34
    His providence, 31
    the mystery of, 54, 58, 59, 61, 63, 64, 131, 139

Trinitarian love, 32, 33, 37, 48, 54, 59
Gospel, the, 20, 24, 33, 34, 53, 54, 66, 74, 75, 93, 104, 106, 110 - 114, 121, 125, 126, 127, 128, 129, 130, 153, 155

H

Hell, 12, 119
Humility, 63
Hypercalvinism, 126

I

Idolatry, 64

J

Joylessness, 115, 138
Judaism, 118

L

Leadership, 98
Liberalism
    modern, 18, 132
Love
    God-centered, 95, 96, 97, 99

M

Man centered religion, 132
Mankind
    limitations of, 54, 58, 64
    sinfulness, 55, 56, 64, 66, 80, 83, 99, 100, 103, 120, 123, 155
Marriage

relevancy of the atonement to, 24
Mishnah, 120, 133

N

nikaō
    Biblical term for victor, 19

P

Pilgrim's Progress, 121
Politics, 103, 105

R

Redemption, 29, 37, 38, 43, 44, 54, 55, 57, 60, 61, 62, 78, 79, 80, 88, 141
Reformation, the, 120

S

Satan, 12, 90
Secularism, 14
Submission, 14

T

Theocentricity, 54, 60
Tradition
    in the church, 15, 16, 17

Pharisees, 13, 17, 75, 76, 119, 120, 121
Trials, 39, 67, 68

U

Unexceptional Love, 106, 108

Universalism, 45, 71, 78, 85, 92, 105

V

Victor
    Christ, the Victorious Lamb, 23, 92, 137, 142, 143

W

Whosoever, as an American theological paradigm, 129, 130, 131, 149, 150
Worship, 12, 15, 24, 25, 26, 40, 61, 62, 76, 86, 90, 92, 94, 128, 129, 136, 141
    devotion to Christ, 29, 30, 90, 92
    the song of the Lamb, 25, 26, 29, 44, 79, 143

Proverbs 3:5-18:

5 Trust in Jehovah with all thy heart, And lean not upon thine own understanding: 6 In all thy ways acknowledge him, And he will direct thy paths. 7 Be not wise in thine own eyes; Fear Jehovah, and depart from evil: 8 It will be health to thy navel, And marrow to thy bones. 9 Honor Jehovah with thy substance, And with the first-fruits of all thine increase: 10 So shall thy barns be filled with plenty, And thy vats shall overflow with new wine. 11 My son, despise not the chastening of Jehovah; Neither be weary of his reproof: 12 For whom Jehovah loveth he reproveth; Even as a father the son in whom he delighteth. 13 Happy is the man that findeth wisdom, And the man that getteth understanding. 14 For the gaining of it is better than the gaining of silver, And the profit thereof than fine gold. 15 She is more precious than rubies: And none of the things thou canst desire are to be compared unto her. 16 Length of days is in her right hand; In her left hand are riches and honor. 17 Her ways are ways of pleasantness, And all her paths are peace. 18 She is a tree of life to them that lay hold upon her: And happy is every one that retaineth her.

www.ingramcontent.com/pod-product-compliance
Lightning Source LLC
Chambersburg PA
CBHW020001050426
42450CB00005B/277